W9-BOE-850

CIVIL RIGHTS MOVEMENT

Sit-Ins and Freedom Rides

CIVIL RIGHTS MOVEMENT

SIT-INS AND FREEDOM RIDES

David Aretha

MORGAN REYNOLDS

PUBLISHING

Greensboro, North Carolina

THE CIVIL RIGHTS MOVEMENT

THE CIVIL RIGHTS MOVEMENT:
SIT-INS AND FREEDOM RIDES

Copyright © 2009 by Morgan Reynolds Publishing

Library of Congress Cataloging-in-Publication Data

Aretha, David.
  Sit-ins and freedom rides / by David Aretha.
    p. cm. -- (Civil rights series)
  Includes bibliographical references and index.
  ISBN-13: 978-1-59935-098-1
  ISBN-10: 1-59935-098-X
  1. African Americans--Civil rights--Southern States--History--20th cen-
tury--Juvenile literature. 2. Civil rights demonstrations--Southern States--
History--20th century--Juvenile literature. 3. Freedom Rides, 1961--Juvenile
literature. 4. Civil rights movements--Southern States--History--20th century-
-Juvenile literature. 5. African American civil rights workers--Southern States-
-History--20th century--Juvenile literature. 6. Civil rights workers--Southern
States--History--20th century--Juvenile literature. 7. Southern States--Race
relations--History--20th century--Juvenile literature. I. Title.
  E185.61.A675 2009
  323.1196'073075--dc22

                                        2008039600

Printed in the United States of America
First Edition

Contents

Students during a sit-in at a segregated Woolworth's lunch counter in Greensboro, North Carolina, that transformed the civil rights movement of the 1960s. *(Courtesy of the News & Record)*

one

Sitting and Riding for Freedom

"**A**t the rate things are going here," wrote African American author James Baldwin, "all of Africa will be free before we can get a lousy cup of coffee."

In 1960, four North Carolina A&T College students pretty much felt the same way. The civil rights movement had begun four years earlier, with a bus boycott in Montgomery, Alabama. But progress was slow. Jim Crow (a euphemism for segregation) continued to reign throughout the South. Due to state and local laws and customs, African Americans were confined to separate and inferior schools, restrooms, restaurants, lunch counters, and more. On February 1, A&T freshmen Ezell Blair, Franklin McCain, David Richmond, and Joseph McNeil—all African American—decided to do their part to force a change.

Dressed in their finest clothes, the four young men entered Woolworth's, a downtown five-and-dime store in Greensboro, North Carolina. African Americans were allowed to purchase items at the store, but they were not allowed to sit at the lunch counter. This was true at lunch counters throughout the South; southern whites did not want to have to eat their food while rubbing shoulders with those whom they saw as the "inferior" race. Nevertheless, after purchasing a few items, the four men took a seat at the "white" lunch counter.

Blair, the leader of the group, politely addressed the waitress behind the counter. "I'd like a cup of coffee, please," he requested.

"I'm sorry," she replied. "We don't serve colored here."

"I beg to disagree with you," Blair replied. "You just finished serving me at a counter only two feet from here." He was referring to the sale of the items.

"Negroes eat on the other end," she said.

"What do you mean?" Blair replied. "This is a public place, isn't it? If it isn't, then why don't you sell membership cards? If you do that, then I'll understand that this is a private concern."

Blair was making sense. The waitress became flustered. "Well you won't get any service here!" she blurted, and then walked away.

Immediately, a young black worker approached the four "troublemakers." "You are stupid, ignorant!" she chastised. "You're dumb! That's why we can't get anywhere today. You know you are supposed to eat at the other end."

The foursome was anything but stupid. They knew that to demolish segregation, they needed to attack it head-on. But they needed to do so politely, lawfully—like gentlemen. If their behavior was impeccable and their cause was just, how could anyone deny them their rights? This form of protest—nonviolent resistance—had been the philosophy of Martin Luther King Jr. and his followers during the Montgomery bus boycott in 1956. In India, Gandhi had utilized this tactic to achieve independence for his people. In fact, a documentary about the legendary Indian leader had inspired Blair to stage the lunch counter sit-in at Woolworth's.

As with Gandhi, Blair's action would profoundly change his nation. The next day, twenty-seven students showed up at Woolworth's, politely demanding service. The day after that, a throng of three hundred protesters arrived. The sit-in movement spread like wildfire throughout the South. Thousands of young people—mostly black, but white too—protested segregated lunch counters at Woolworth's, Kress, and countless other establishments. Other civil rights activists staged sit-ins at other segregated public facilities: libraries, museums, swimming pools, and more.

In the spring of 1961, groups of men and women—called Freedom Riders—took the sit-in tactic on the road. A year earlier, the U.S. Supreme Court had ruled that racial segregation in public transportation (and facilities, such as bus terminals) was illegal. Yet in 1961, "WHITE" and "COLORED" signs still hung next to bus terminal waiting rooms throughout the South. As they had since the Civil War, and before, white Southerners were defying race-related federal laws.

In May 1961, thirteen civil rights activists—most from the Congress of Racial Equality (CORE)—decided to test the ruling. Boarding Greyhound and Trailways buses, they journeyed from Washington, D.C., to the Deep South. In Rock Hill, South Carolina, two of these Freedom Riders—John Lewis (black) and Al Bigelow (white)—entered a Greyhound terminal. Trouble was imminent.

Rock Hill, a small factory town, teemed with Ku Klux Klansmen. Moreover, racial tensions had been smoldering in Rock Hill for more than a year due to the multiple sit-ins that had occurred there. Above the white waiting room, a "WHITE" sign still hung. Two young white men, dressed in leather jackets and smoking cigarettes, addressed Lewis as he attempted to enter the room.

"Other side, nigger," one of the men said while pointing to a waiting room sign that said "COLORED."

"I have a right to go in there," Lewis said about the white-designated waiting room while maintaining his composure, "on the grounds of the Supreme Court decision in the *Boynton* case."

One of the men cursed at Lewis. "The next thing I knew, a fist smashed the right side of my head," Lewis wrote. "Then another hit me square in the face. As I fell to the floor I could feel feet kicking me hard in the sides. I could taste blood in my mouth."

Bigelow, a big, powerful man, stepped into the middle of the fracas. He threw no punches, for CORE members were also dedicated to nonviolence. He simply tried to shield Lewis from more blows. The men responded by punching Bigelow, dropping him to one knee. More local whites joined the melee. When Freedom Rider Genevieve Hughes got in their way, they knocked her to the floor. A white police officer, who had watched the fighting with the patience of a hockey referee, finally stepped in. "All right, boys," he said. "Y'all've done about enough now. Get on home."

After events like this, many took the next bus back to Washington. But these Freedom Riders were on a mission—to hammer away at racial injustice. Freedom Riders from CORE and later the Student Nonviolent Coordinating Committee (SNCC) would continue to desegregate southern facilities in

Members of the Washington Freedom Riders Committee display signs protesting segregation as they travel from New York to Washington, D.C., in 1961. *(Library of Congress)*

the spring and summer of 1961. Segregationists would beat them with baseball bats, metal chains, and iron pipes, and a bomb would destroy one of their buses. But they continued to ride.

Like the sit-in demonstrators, the Freedom Riders would profoundly change the laws and customs of America. They would not only desegregate much of the South themselves, but they would inspire and embolden thousands of other Americans to join the fight for civil rights.

two

Jim Crow Has to Go

Born in 1910, Pauli Murray grew up as an orphan in Durham, North Carolina. She lived next to a cemetery, but the worst part of her childhood was living under the ominous specter of Jim Crow.

"Our seedy run-down school told us that if we had any place at all in the scheme of things it was a separate place, marked off, proscribed and unwanted by the white people," Murray wrote. "We were bottled up and labeled and set aside—sent to the Jim Crow car, the back of the bus, the side door of the theater, the side window of a restaurant. We came to understand that whatever we had was always inferior."

Originally, Jim Crow was a bumbling black caricature made popular in minstrel shows in the mid-1800s. But by the turn of the century, the term was used as an adjective in the South. "Jim Crow laws" meant "segregation laws." From the 1860s to the 1960s, southern legislatures created codes and then laws that marginalized black citizens. In the Jim Crow South, whites constructed a racial caste system in which they maintained supreme power. Their jobs, wages, schools, homes, roads, lodging, and restrooms were all superior to those of blacks.

White Southerners dominated government and law enforcement, which gave them complete control. Through (unconstitutional) laws, as well as intimidation, they prevented most black citizens from voting. Those "nigras" who "stepped out of line" faced severe punishment—harsh jail sentences, firings, severe beatings, or worse. From 1880 to 1950, more than 3,000 African Americans were lynched in the South.

Jim Crow's influence extended as far north as the nation's capital. Aspiring ballplayer Hank Aaron found that out in 1952 while playing in the Negro Leagues (themselves a segregated creation). A white restaurant in Washington, D.C., did serve the all-black Indianapolis Clowns that day, but the workers let their feelings be known. The future home run king wrote:

> I can still envision sitting with the Clowns in a restaurant behind Griffith Stadium and hearing them break all the plates in the kitchen after we were finished eating. What a horrible sound. Even as a kid [of eighteen], the irony hit me: Here we were in the capital in the land of freedom and equality, and they had to destroy the plates that had touched the forks that had been in the mouths of black men. If dogs had eaten off those plates, they'd have washed them.

Southern segregation had its roots, of course, in slavery. From 1619 until the end of the Civil War, white Southerners owned blacks as slaves, breaking up their families, forcing them to work for free, and depriving them of human rights and dignity. Although the South was never a wealthy region, many white landowners lived comfortable lives thanks to the free labor of their Negro slaves. To psychologically justify this cruel mistreatment of human beings, whites branded the African race as inferior. Many considered black people as sub-human, hopelessly ignorant, and not worthy of God's love.

To preserve slavery and its economic advantages, southern states seceded from the Union and fought the Civil War to the bitter end. Southern whites were enraged by President Abraham Lincoln's Emancipation Proclamation, in which he declared "that all persons held as slaves" within the rebellious southern states "henceforward shall be free." To many white Southerners, January 31, 1865, was a dark day. That is when Congress passed the Thirteenth Amendment to the Constitution, officially abolishing slavery.

A large group of slaves on a South Carolina plantation in 1862 *(Library of Congress)*

From 1865 to 1877, the South experienced a volatile period known as Reconstruction. During that time, the federal government tried to reintegrate the southern states into the United States while granting full citizenship rights to the black people of America. Regarding the latter, Congress fulfilled its intentions. In 1868, it passed the Fourteenth Amendment, which granted full citizenship to all people born or naturalized in the United States. In 1870, Congress passed the Fiftheenth Amendment, which guaranteed voting rights to all adult male citizens. African Americans were further encouraged by the passing of the Civil Rights Act of 1875, which prohibited discrimination in public facilities. During Reconstruction, black males ("Freedmen") cast votes and took political office.

But while the Republicans (the party of Abraham Lincoln) imposed their equal-rights agenda, southern white Democrats challenged them at every step. In the mid- to late 1860s, southern legislatures enacted "black codes." According to these new rules, black Americans could not rent land, serve on juries, learn to read, bear arms, travel, drink alcohol, or assemble except for religious purposes. In the 1870s, white Democrats strengthened their political power in the South. White terror organizations, such as the Ku Klux Klan and the White League, prevented black Southerners from voting, often through intimidation and violence.

Economically, southern blacks remained virtually enslaved. In the practice of sharecropping, plantation owners rented their land to black men, who harvested and sold their crops. However, the workers had to pay so much to the plantation owners—for farming equipment, rent, and food—that they were chronically in debt.

A Ku Klux Klan rally in 1921. The Klan used tactics of terror and intimidation to help enforce Jim Crow laws across the South. *(Library of Congress)*

The U.S. Supreme Court became a foe of African Americans, reversing their earlier gains. In 1876, the court ruled that citizens could be denied the right to vote if they did not meet certain criteria. Seven years later, it ruled that while *states* were constitutionally bound to respect the rights of black Americans, *individuals* were not obligated to do so. Thus, if restaurant owners did not want to serve black people, they didn't have to.

Beginning in 1870, southern state legislatures passed their first Jim Crow laws. In Tennessee that year, lawmakers mandated the separation of black and white riders on trains. Up through the mid-1900s, southern legislatures continued to pass Jim Crow laws, separating the races. In virtually all instances, the black facilities received less money and were of inferior quality. States segregated railway cars, streetcars,

A family of impoverished sharecroppers on the porch of their North Carolina home in 1939. *(Library of Congress)*

theater seats, outhouses, drinking fountains, laundries, and more. The minutia of the laws was extraordinary. In Atlanta, black witnesses could not swear on the same Bible as whites. In South Carolina, blacks and whites could not look out the same factory window together.

In the Jim Crow world, blacks had to call white men "mister" while whites called black men "boy." Black schools (in many cases just one-room shacks) were so inferior that African Americans couldn't possibly receive a good education. White

A 1916 photo of a segregated African American school in Kentucky. *(Library of Congress)*

men were so threatened by the sexuality of black men ("black bucks," as white men referred to them) that they passed such laws as "reckless eyeballing," which stated that a black man could go to jail if he looked at a white woman the wrong way. Rumors of a black man raping a white woman triggered horrific riots in Tulsa, Oklahoma (1921), Rosewood, Florida (1923), and other places. In reality, black men very rarely solicited white women; they understood the repercussions.

The U.S. Supreme Court case *Plessy* v. *Ferguson* (1896) legitimized southern segregation. The court ruled that separate-but-equal facilities were constitutional. Over the subsequent decades, *equal* became a subjective and largely unenforceable term. Jim Crow stood strong for years, even into the 1960s.

There were many reasons why many white Southerners were so determined and went to so much trouble to keep power away from blacks. Certainly, tradition had much to do with it. The South had maintained a rigid racial caste system since the 1600s, and attitudes were passed from one generation to the next. Many whites believed that they were a superior race. To them, granting equal rights to "inferiors" made little sense.

Moreover, sex had much to do with the continuation of Jim Crow. Whites not only feared the "defilement" of their "white maidens," but they dreaded the "mongrelization" of the human race. Senator Theodore Bilbo (D-Mississippi, 1935-47) believed that biracial children were mongrels—a mixed and inferior breed. Moreover, many whites believed that biracial citizens would upset the black-white caste system that they wanted to maintain.

Whites' education—or lack of it—was another reason that segregation was perpetuated. Much of the South was rural, and a relatively small percentage of southern whites went to college. In addition, their textbooks were "white-washed." That is, the books glorified whites, espoused the southern-white agenda, and ignored the accomplishments and concerns of African Americans.

Power and money also explain why Jim Crow remained so healthy for so long. If black citizens attained equal opportunities in the South, whites wouldn't be able to hire them for low wages. Moreover, African Americans would become competitors for their jobs. Thus, keeping black Americans "in their place" kept the white South's economy afloat.

In Mississippi, the most segregated state in the nation, more African Americans than whites lived in the state until the 1930s. White Mississippians felt that if pure democracy rang in their state, black citizens would elect black politicians.

Theoretically, African Americans would (or at least could) rule the state—an unbearable thought for the state's white citizenry. As Alabama governor George Wallace declared in 1962, "I say segregation now, segregation tomorrow, segregation forever!"

With segregation firmly entrenched, black Southerners had few options outside of enduring a life of hardship. One thing they could do was leave the South, and many did. During the first Great Migration (1910-40), more than 1.5 million African Americans migrated to the North and West, where factory jobs were plentiful. In the Second Great Migration (1940-70), another 5 million left the South for better lives.

But the millions of African Americans who remained in the South learned that they could not rely solely on the federal government to dismantle segregation. Many northern congressmen cared little about civil rights. This was especially true during the Great Depression (1930s) and World War II (1939-45), when the president and Congress dealt with more pressing needs. Moreover, southern congressmen fiercely opposed any legislation that favored desegregation. Even anti-lynching bills—which simply proposed that lynching should be a federal crime—couldn't get passed due to southern opposition. Senator Bilbo opposed one such bill in 1938. "If you succeed in the passage of this bill," he declared, "you will open the floodgates of hell in the South. Raping, mobbing, lynching, race riots, and crime will be increased a thousandfold."

African Americans realized that if they wanted to destroy Jim Crow, they would have to force the issue themselves. In the early 1900s, some activists began to fight for civil rights. In 1909, black and white progressives formed the National Association for the Advancement of Colored People

Signs that relegated African Americans to using separate facilities were common throughout the Jim Crow South. *(Library of Congress)*

(NAACP). Their mission was to "ensure the political, educational, social, and economic equality of rights of all persons and to eliminate racial hatred and racial discrimination." In 1913, the NAACP actively opposed racial segregation in the federal government. Over the years, the organization focused on anti-lynching legislation, black disenfranchisement, and the desegregation of public schools. The NAACP's biggest success came in the 1954 *Brown* v. *Board of Education* decision, when the U.S. Supreme Court ruled that segregation in public schools was unconstitutional.

In the mid-1930s, an organized protest campaign—similar to the sit-ins—emerged in the Midwest and the East. It was called the "Don't Buy Where You Can't Work" campaign. African Americans boycotted white stores that did not hire black workers. New York City activist Adam Clayton Powell told his people: "It's in your hands. Just like little David had those smooth stones and killed big Goliath with them. Use what you have right in your hand. That dollar . . . that ten cents. Use your vote. The Negro race has enough power right in our hands to accomplish anything we want to."

In the 1950s, anti-segregation boycotts emerged in the South. In 1953, Reverend T. J. Jemison staged a successful bus boycott in Baton Rouge, Louisiana. After five days, the city agreed to an open-seating policy. In Montgomery, Alabama, in 1956-57, Jemison gave advice to Reverend Martin Luther King Jr. during the Montgomery bus boycott. That protest, sparked by Rosa Park's refusal to yield her bus seat to a white man, lasted 381 days and launched the modern civil rights movement. A similar bus boycott was staged in Tallahassee, Florida, in 1956-57.

Though these protests chipped away at segregation, Jim Crow continued to rule in the South in the late 1950s. "Colored" signs still hung in restaurants in Birmingham, Alabama, in bus stations in Jackson, Mississippi, and all throughout the South. In general, southern whites fiercely opposed integration. In the mid-1950s, White Citizens' Councils (WCC) arose in the southern states. Their mission was to maintain segregation through economic intimidation. If WCC members felt that a black man was a threat to white supremacy, they found ways to get him fired or ruin him financially.

Whites strongly resisted the integration of public schools (as mandated by *Brown*), resulting in numerous confrontations.

Black students arrive at a newly integrated school in Clinton, Tennessee, as a crowd of white students looks on. *(Library of Congress)*

In 1956, whites hurled rocks and eggs at Autherine Lucy as she tried to become the first black student at the University of Alabama. At Little Rock's Central High School in 1957, whites spat at and tore the clothing of African American student Elizabeth Eckford. President Dwight Eisenhower had to call in the National Guard to allow the "Little Rock Nine" to attend classes. Said Alfred Williams, one of the first black students at a high school in Clinton, Tennessee, "You couldn't possibly get anything learned or done because you were constantly afraid that the white kid next to you was planning to kill you."

On September 9, 1957, President Eisenhower signed the Civil Rights Act of 1957. The act established a civil rights division within the Justice Department and called for the creation of the U.S. Commission on Civil Rights. It also allowed the U.S. government to bring a lawsuit against anyone interfering with another citizen's right to vote. Practically, the new legislation did virtually nothing to end segregation or black disenfranchisement. On the very day that the act was signed, whites detonated a bomb at a newly integrated elementary school in Nashville, Tennessee.

Though the Greensboro Four started the sit-in movement on February 1, 1960, other civil rights activists staged sit-ins prior to that date. Though their efforts received little media attention at the time, they are historically noteworthy.

In 1942, the Congress of Racial Equality (CORE) was founded in Chicago. Founders James Farmer, George Houser, and Bernice Fisher sought to use nonviolent tactics to dismantle segregation. CORE launched a sit-in in Chicago in 1943. On May 14, twenty-six CORE activists poured in to the Jack Spratt Coffee Shop near the University of Chicago. Farmer had known from experience that Jack Spratt had racist policies, and on this day he tested that theory.

The coffee shop's employees were shocked to see the racially mixed group fill up all of the counter seats and available booths. The activists did nothing except sit down and wait for service. At first, the managers offered to serve the men and women if they agreed to move to the basement. "I told them we were comfortable where we were," Farmer said. "They served us."

In 1943, Patricia Harris and Pauli Murray—students at all-black Howard University—tested the segregation policies of the Little Palace cafeteria. Though the neighborhood was mostly African American, the restaurant was whites-only. The protest resulted in the desegregation of the restaurant; Howard students, for the first time, were allowed service.

From 1943 through 1959, more than a dozen sit-ins were held across the country. In Wichita, Kansas, and Oklahoma City, Oklahoma, in summer 1958, the NAACP Youth Council considered holding sit-ins at segregated lunch counters. Though the NAACP would not sanction the sit-ins, the young activists proceeded anyway.

In July 1958, Youth Council members Carol Parks-Haun, nineteen, and cousin Ron Walters, twenty, planned a sit-in at Dockum Drugstore in Wichita. Up to that time, only white people had enjoyed meals and soda fountain drinks at the drugstore's lunch counter. Other Wichita eateries were seg-regated, but, said Walters, "we deliberately chose Dockum because Dockum was part of a chain—the Rexall Drugstore chain—and we felt if we could do something there in the heart of town, it might have a consequence."

Haun sat down on a lunch counter stool and ordered a Coke. She recalled: "She gave it to me and I said, 'oh my,' and the others came in and they sat and she looked at them—and she looked at me—and she leaned forward and she said, 'You are not colored, are you, dear?' And I said, 'Oh yes, I am,' and then she pulled away.' She pulled back because the store policy was not to serve colored people."

For three weeks, Youth Council students quietly sat at the lunch counter, up to hours at a time. Still, the waiters refused to serve them. Adhering to sit-in protocol, the protesters ignored the words of those who taunted them. After four weeks, the store's owner made a pronouncement. Parks-Haun remembered: "He came to the door and he looked directly to his manager and he said, 'Serve them—I'm losing too much money,' and then he left. It was that simple."

Because the local media chose not to cover the story, the Wichita sit-in became lost in history. So too did the Oklahoma

African Americans sitting at a segregated lunch counter in Oklahoma City, Oklahoma, in 1958. *(Library of Congress)*

City sit-in. Clara Luper, the first African American ever admitted to the University of Oklahoma history department, was working as a teacher at Dunjee High School. On August 19, 1958, Luper and thirteen NAACP Youth Council members initiated a sit-in at the Katz Drugstore counter. After requesting service and being denied, Luper and the teens refused to leave. Whites in the restaurant were outraged. They cursed the protesters, spat on them, and threw food and drinks at them. Police arrived and hauled the protesters away. The group's bravery sparked other civil rights demonstrations in Oklahoma, though those also weren't met with much success.

The year 1959 was a quiet one for civil rights, but it served as a "training camp" of sorts for the combative decade to come. In February 1959, Martin Luther King Jr. traveled to India to study Gandhi's principles of nonviolent resistance. Also that year, CORE and the Fellowship of Reconciliation (FOR) conducted workshops in the South on nonviolent protests. In April 1959, CORE staged sit-ins at lunch counters in downtown Miami. Up to fifty activists participated at each.

CORE'S Gordon Carey wrote of a September protest at Jackson's-Byrons Department Store in Miami: "Six days of continuous sit-ins caused the owners of the lunch counter concession to close temporarily while considering a change of policy." On September 19, the owners of Jackson's-Byrons promised to serve African Americans, but then they reneged. In late September, dozens of CORE protesters continued sit-ins in Miami. Some were arrested while others were physically attacked. Grant's Department Store closed rather than serve African Americans.

The Miami sit-ins also escaped national attention. However, many young black activists—in CORE, NAACP Youth Councils, and black universities—were becoming aware of the sporadic protests. In Greensboro, North Carolina, four college freshmen decided that they too wanted to make a difference. On the first day of February in 1960, they pushed open the door at Woolworth's and changed the nation forever.

three

The Greensboro Sit-ins

It all started with a hot dog.

During Christmas vacation in 1959, Joseph McNeil took a Greyhound bus from New York City to the Greensboro bus terminal. The North Carolina A&T freshman had just returned from winter break. Before going to his dormitory, he decided to order a hot dog. He was denied; they did not serve Negroes at the Greensboro bus terminal.

For McNeil, this was the last straw. He had grown up in Wilmington, North Carolina, attending that city's Williston High School. But after graduating, he moved to New York City, where he experienced freedoms that he had never experienced in the Jim Crow South. An outstanding student, McNeil earned a full scholarship to North Carolina A&T. Though he may have been happy with the all-black college, he could not tolerate the racist society around him.

"I had lived in New York," he recalled, "and when I went back down there to school I realized the transition, the difference in public accommodations. . . . It seemed to me that people in Alabama, where they had the Montgomery bus boycott, were at least trying to do something about it. The people in Little Rock, with the trouble at Central High School, were trying to do something. And we weren't."

McNeil, of course, wasn't the only frustrated student at the school. His roommate, Ezell Blair Jr., came from a politically active family. His father, an NAACP member, had made him well aware of the racism that pervaded their society. Blair attended Dudley High School in Greensboro, a segregated

Ezell Blair Jr. (center) talks with Dr. George Simkins (right), a Greensboro dentist and local NAACP leader, and Joseph McNeil (left). *(Courtesy of AP Images)*

(all-black) school, where he befriended David Richmond. Richmond excelled athletically at Dudley, setting the state record in the high jump. But he, like Blair, had other barriers he wanted to clear.

In 1958, Blair and Richmond ventured to Bennett College in Greensboro to hear the guest speaker, Martin Luther King Jr. Blair, for one, was enthralled. King discussed the times that he had to ride in the back of the bus because of his race. Though he sat in the rear seats, King said, his mind was always up front. King's speech profoundly affected Blair. He said he could feel his heart thumping, and tears welled in his eyes.

At Dudley High School, Blair also became friends with Franklin McCain, who had moved to Greensboro from Washington, D.C. McCain also was mad and frustrated with his segregated community. In 1959, Blair, Richmond, and McCain made the transition from Dudley to North Carolina A&T. Blair wound up sharing a room in Scott Hall with McNeil, who became friends with the Dudley threesome. Together, they would become immortalized as the Greensboro Four.

Each of the Four had been NAACP Youth Council members, and at least one had read a copy of *Martin Luther King and the Montgomery Story*. This comic book, produced by the Fellowship of Reconciliation, included instructions for nonviolent resistance against segregation. For the Greensboro Four, a lifetime of prejudice, the successes of the civil rights movement over the previous four years, and McNeil's humiliating experience at the bus terminal prompted them to take action. On January 31, 1960, the foursome sat down and wrote a letter, which they signed "Students Executive Committee for Justice." The next day, they took justice into their own hands.

Franklin McCain (left) and David Richmond, two of the Greensboro Four. *(Courtesy of AP Images)*

It was approximately 4:30 p.m. when Blair, McNeil, McCain, and Richmond entered Woolworth's on North Elm Street. First they purchased a few items, including toothpaste and notebook paper, at the checkout counter. Then they sat on the stools of the lunch counter, which everyone knew were reserved for white patrons. This was not just a bold act but a dangerous one too. The young men knew that sit-in demonstrators in other cities had been arrested and sent to jail. And jail was a frightening place to be for black men who had threatened white supremacy. Jailers were known to physically abuse black "upstarts."

Nevertheless, the young men took their seats. Each ordered coffee and, according to McNeil, a slice of apple pie. McCain recalled the euphoria he felt shortly after he sat on the stool:

> Fifteen seconds after . . . I had the most wonderful feeling. I had a feeling of liberation, restored manhood. I had a natural high. And I truly felt almost invincible. . . . We advised the store and its employees and its manager [that] we intended to sit and continue to sit until they served us. . . . The store manager called the police, and the policeman came and he walked back and forth behind us. And he took his nightstick and he thumped it in his hand in a threatening manner, but we continued to sit.

An older white woman sat at the lunch counter, several stools down from the four black men. When the woman looked their way, McCain assumed that only racist thoughts were swirling through her head. When she finished her doughnut and coffee, she walked up to McCain and McNeil and put her hands on their shoulders. McCain recalled: "She said in a very calm voice, 'Boys, I am so proud of you. I only regret that you didn't do this ten years ago.'"

McCain was pleasantly stunned. "What I learned from that little incident was . . . don't you ever, ever stereotype anybody in this life until you at least experience them and have the opportunity to talk to them," he said.

The foursome sat, unserved, for more than a half hour. "They can just sit there," store manager Clarence Harris said. "It's nothing to me." They sat until 5:30, when Harris closed the store. They walked out proudly, for they had just staged their first civil rights protest. "I can't even describe it,"

McCain said. "Never have I experienced such an incredible emotion, such an uplift."

The Greensboro Four felt so uplifted that they returned the next day. And this time, they brought company. After they had contacted A&T's student body president, many other students volunteered for the February 2 sit-in. All total, twenty A&T students arrived at Woolworth's at 10:30 the next morning. Each made a small purchase, and then they sat at the lunch counter in groups of threes and fours—depending on the availability of seats. For more than an hour and a half,

The Greensboro Four leaving Woolworth after the first day of the sit-in. From left to right: David Richmond, Franklin McCain, Ezell Blair, and Joseph McNeil. *(Courtesy of the* [Greensboro] News & Record)

they waited for service that never came. There were no disturbances, and some of the protesters pulled out books and began to study. They stayed until after noon, then ended their protest with a prayer.

Marvin Sykes, a reporter for the *Greensboro Record,* covered the story. Clarence Harris, the Woolworth manager, wouldn't speak to the press. Ezell Blair, however, had plenty to say. He declared that African American adults "have been complacent and fearful. . . . It is time for someone to wake up and change the situation . . . and we decided to start here."

Dr. George Simkins, head of the local chapter of the NAACP, said that his organization had nothing to do with the sit-in. But, he added, "if any legal action arises as a result, the NAACP is prepared to back the group."

Besides the local press, a national news service ran a story of the protest. By the next day, Wednesday, February 3, the

A group of North Carolina A&T students who were refused service on the second day of the Woolworth sit-in. *(Library of Congress)*

sit-ins were the talk of the town. More students arrived at the Woolworth's store. Reported the *Record*: "No service was given. More Negro students waited in the aisle to take the place of the students who left."

Hundreds of demonstrators arrived on Wednesday and Thursday. The *Register,* A&T's student newspaper, quoted one eager participant in its Thursday edition: "The doors opened and in we went. I almost ran, because I was determined to get a seat and I was very much interested in being the first to sit down. I sat down and there was a waitress standing directly in front of me, so I asked her if I might have a cup of black coffee and two donuts please. She looked at me and moved on to another area."

On Wednesday, the protest stretched beyond the boundaries of A&T. Three white Greensboro College students joined the demonstrators: Lowell Lott, Ed Bryant, and Rick O'Neal. North Carolina attorney general Malcolm Seawell issued a statement, declaring that a private business had the legal right to deny service to customers of their choosing. In New York, a spokesman for the F. W. Woolworth Company said it was their policy to abide by local custom. But W. H. Gamble, dean of men at A&T, displayed implicit support for the protesters. He said that the school had no authority to restrict students' private activities.

During the latter part of the week, sit-ins continued at Woolworth's as well as the lunch counter at S. H. Kress & Co., a five-and-dime store across the street. Hundreds of young African Americans participated, and white youth began to heckle the activists. Certainly the sit-in participation of three white Woman's College students did not sit well with white males. Confrontations became particularly heated on Saturday. Then, after a bomb threat that day, both

Woolworth's and Kress officials announced that they were closing their lunch counters indefinitely. On Saturday night, A&T students stated that they would halt their sit-ins for two weeks to allow time for negotiations.

On Saturday, Mayor George Roach called for a peaceful solution. Roach pointed out in his Saturday address that Greensboro had already desegregated its bus system, parks, libraries, and airport, as well as some of its schools. Some city facilities, however, had yet to be fully desegregated, including swimming pools. (During the civil rights movement, many whites strongly resisted sharing pool water with African Americans.) Of course, A&T students felt that all forms of segregation were degrading, oppressive, and unconstitutional, and that all should be eliminated.

Despite the cooling-off period in Greensboro, sit-in demonstrations sprouted in other parts of the country. On Monday, February 8, sit-in protests began in Charlotte, North Carolina, and later in the week they spread across the state. With their February 1 sit-in, the Greensboro Four had sparked a wildfire—one that was about to spread throughout the South.

The events in Greensboro encouraged civil rights veterans to take action. Reverend Ralph Abernathy, who had been Martin Luther King Jr.'s right-hand man during the Montgomery bus boycott, hosted Alabama State College students at his home as they planned upcoming sit-ins. Daisy Bates, who had spearheaded the desegregation of Central High School in Little Rock, helped recruit sit-in protesters.

SCLC member Fred Shuttlesworth, who had attempted a bus boycott in Birmingham in 1956, also became involved. He contacted Ella Baker, the SCLC's executive director. "You must tell Martin [Luther King] that we must get with this," he told Baker, adding that the sit-ins might "shake up the world."

A longtime activist, Baker reached out to her friends on southern campuses. "What are you going to do?" she asked. "It's time to move."

Gordon Carey, who had overseen previous sit-ins for CORE, flew to North Carolina to help the cause there. Though largely forgotten today, Carey was an unsung hero of the sit-in movement. He taught sit-in tactics to students in multiple cities, thus contributing greatly to the spread of the protests.

Fred Shuttlesworth (*Library of Congress*)

While partaking in a sit-in, demonstrators had to follow certain rules. They needed to be polite and friendly at all times. They were supposed to sit straight and always face the counter. They should not laugh or hold conversations with anyone. They should not respond to any insults and slurs. Even if whites hurled food and drinks at them (which did happen at some sit-ins), they should remain calm. If arrested, they should go to jail without resistance.

If the protesters remained dignified, authorities would have no good reason to arrest them. Moreover, their dignified manner (coupled with their noble cause) would likely garner empathy from the nation's citizens and Washington's politicians. This was critically important because the ultimate goal of civil rights leaders was the passage of strong federal legislation that would wipe out Jim Crow practices once and for all.

James J. Kilpatrick, editor of the *Richmond News Leader* in Virginia, was a noted segregationist. However, he admitted that the African American protesters looked far more respectable than those who tried to harass them. He wrote: "Here were the colored students, in coats, white shirts, ties, and one of them was reading Goethe and one was taking notes from a biology text. And here, on the sidewalk outside, was a gang of white boys come to heckle, a ragtail rabble, slack-jawed, black-jacketed, grinning fit to kill, and some of them, God save the mark, were waving the proud and honored flag of the Southern states in the last war fought by gentlemen. . . . Eheu! It gives one pause."

By mid-February, students were holding sit-ins in eleven cities, mostly at Woolworth's and Kress stores. In Tallahassee, both black and white students of Florida Agricultural and Mechanical University held a sit-in at a Woolworth's. Sit-in leaders agreed that it was best to target those large national chains. If they could convince company executives to change their lunch counter policies, then all the Woolworth's and Kress stores throughout the South could instantly become desegregated. But students held sit-ins in other places too.

The threat of a sit-in made southern storeowners nervous. Some placed signs in their windows, such as "No Trespassing" and "We Reserve the Right to Service the Public as We See Fit." While many southern whites vehemently opposed lunch counter segregation, some began to show their support. On February 19, the North Carolina Council of Churches endorsed the sit-ins. The organization recognized "the democratic and moral right of Negroes to equality of service at the lunch counters of stores serving the public."

On February 19 and 20, the Associated Press reported on sit-ins in Raleigh, North Carolina, and the picketing of a

Woolworth's in New Haven, Connecticut. At the latter demonstration, Yale University students handed out leaflets that declared: "We are attempting to communicate to others that Woolworth's branches in Greensboro, Raleigh, Fayetteville and Durham, N.C., like many other Southern stores, treat their Negro customers undemocratically and deny to them the same seated meal service provided to white people."

Few southern whites shared the Ivy League idealism. In Rock Hill, South Carolina, whites threw ammonia at sit-in demonstrators. At other establishments, angry locals tossed "itching powder" at the activists. In Raleigh, forty-three

Martin Luther King Jr. (front, center) at a 1960 conference about a sit-in movement in Raleigh, North Carolina. *(Courtesy of Donald Uhrbrock/Time & Life Pictures/Getty Images)*

protesters at a Woolworth's were arrested for trespassing. They posted fifty-dollar bonds and were released.

For African Americans, these "battle wounds" were a small price to pay for their cause. Activists were trying to crush a system of oppression that had lasted for more than three hundred years. The A&T students were well aware of the profound nature of their efforts. In a letter to North Carolina attorney general Malcolm Seawall, they wrote: "Negroes, who are also citizens of North Carolina, can no longer remain quiet and complacent and continue to accept such gross injustices from those who desire no change in old customs and traditions solely for the purpose of personal gain or because the warped ideas which have been instilled in the minds of many responsible citizens."

Martin Luther King Jr. also recognized the epic (and unique) nature of the sit-in movement. At a rally in North Carolina on February 16, he declared: "What is fresh, what is new in your fight is the fact that it was initiated, led, and sustained by students. What is new is that American students have come of age. You now take your honored places in the worldwide struggle for freedom."

As King was speaking, that worldwide struggle was spreading to another southern city. Those surprised by the size of the Greensboro movement were shocked by the turn-outs in Nashville, Tennessee.

four

"Ins" Across the South

With thirteen colleges and universities, Nashville was billed as a progressive city. Much of Nashville had already been desegregated. African Americans attended integrated public schools, shared seats with white people on city buses, and worked on the city council and police force. However, theaters, hotels, libraries, restaurants, and lunch counters remained segregated. James Lawson, a thirty-one-year-old black theology student at Vanderbilt University, wanted to obliterate all forms of segregation in Nashville—and soon.

Like Martin Luther King Jr., Lawson had traveled to India to study the nonviolent movement of Gandhi. In 1959, Lawson and fellow activists staged workshops on nonviolence with the goal of desegregating Nashville's downtown establishments. Students from various universities as well as some adults attended weekly meetings.

In November 1959, those in the workshops participated in small sit-ins—three or four people at a restaurant. Their sit-ins were different than those in Greensboro. "[T]hey were not supposed to be arrested," Lawson said. "They were supposed to sit, ask for service, and if it did not come—which of course it didn't—then talk with customers around them, and talk with the waiter, waitresses, see what their attitudes were, and then ask to see the manager or somebody in authority and talk with them about the policy of the place."

On February 3, Douglas Moore—a North Carolina minister involved in the Greensboro sit-ins—phoned Lawson. Moore told him that the sit-ins were beginning to spread to other cities, and he urged Lawson to do his part. Lawson concurred, and on Friday, February 12, he held a mass meeting at Nashville's First Baptist Church. People were so eager to be part of the new sit-in movement that five hundred showed up at the meeting.

Seventy-five of the attendees were veterans of Lawson's workshops, but the rest knew virtually nothing about sit-in tactics. Lawson gave them a crash course on the dos and don'ts. He talked about what to wear, how to avoid loitering laws, how to take a person's spot when that person had to go to the bathroom, and so on. Lawson and the adults wanted to hold off on mass sit-ins until the protesters were properly trained. They also were concerned about mass arrests. The Nashville Christian Leadership Conference (NCLC), an affiliate of the SCLC, had very little money to spend on bail. Nevertheless, the students were eager to get started right away.

The next morning, on Saturday, February 13, a large number of well-dressed activists returned to First Baptist Church. From there, they broke into smaller groups and headed to downtown establishments. They went to the five-and-

Smoke is blown in the face of a lunch counter protester during a sit-in training session. *(Courtesy of Howard Sochurek/Time Life Pictures/Getty Images)*

dime stores that belonged to national chains—Woolworth's, Kresge's, and McClellan's. They entered the stores at about 12:30 and sat at the lunch counters. The employees refused to serve them, but they continued to sit, not leaving until two hours later.

Diane Nash was among the leaders of the Nashville sit-in movement. Raised in Chicago, Nash attended Fisk University in Nashville, where she felt degraded by the city's segregation. She attended Lawson's workshops in 1959 and helped orchestrate the February 13 demonstrations. She recalled: "The first sit-in we had was really funny. The waitresses were nervous. They must have dropped $2,000 worth of dishes that day. . . . It was almost like a cartoon . . . we were sitting there trying not to laugh [but] at the same time we were scared to death."

Students from Fisk University participating in a sit-in in Nashville, Tennessee. *(Library of Congress)*

The second Nashville sit-in, on February 18, was bigger than the first. More than two hundred students entered Woolworth's, Kresge's, McClellan's, and Grant's. The store-owners responded by closing the counters, and the protesters remained for about an hour before leaving. On February 20, more than three hundred students entered the aforementioned stores as well as the Walgreens drugstore. At Walgreens, the owners put up a sign that said, "Fountain Closed in Interest of Public Safety." Employees even placed rugs and flowerpots on the counter so that the demonstrators couldn't study.

The repeated sit-ins eventually pushed white citizens passed the breaking point. On February 27, on a beautiful day in Nashville, large numbers of students staged sit-ins downtown. They had been warned that trouble awaited them, and sure enough, it did. According to participant (and future U.S.

During the course of the sit-in movement, many lunch counters closed in an attempt to avoid controversy. Here, protesters sit at a Nashville lunch counter that has been "closed in the interest of public safety." *(Courtesy of Lynn Pelham/Time Life Pictures/Getty Images)*

congressman) John Lewis, police officers allowed "a group of white hoodlums and thugs [to] come in and beat people up."

After the demonstrators took up all the seats in the Woolworth's, Lewis recalled: "A group of young white men came in and they started pulling and beating primarily the young women. They put lighted cigarettes down their backs, in their hair, and they were really beating people."

Shortly afterward, police arrived and arrested people—not the white attackers but the peaceful demonstrators. It happened in waves. First, everyone at the lunch counter was arrested and sent to the paddy wagon. When they left the stools, another round of protesters sat down at the counter. Recalled Nash: "[The police] were confounded and kind of looked at each other like, 'Now what do we do,' you know? And they said, 'Well, okay, we'll arrest those too,' and they did it and then the third wave. And no matter what they did and how many they arrested, there was still a lunch counter full of students there."

All told that day, police arrested eighty-one student demonstrators. The black adults in Nashville rallied to their

A group of Nashville students eating in jail after being arrested for protesting lunch counter discrimination. *(Courtesy of Lynn Pelham/Time Life Pictures/Getty Images)*

cause, raising $50,000 for bail money. On February 29, black attorney Z. Alexander Looby represented the students in a Nashville courtroom. When Looby spoke to defend his clients, the judge literally turned his back to him. When he finally turned around, the judge declared the students guilty of disorderly conduct and fined them $150 plus court costs.

The arrests did not discourage the protesters. On March 2, more than sixty were arrested while holding a sit-in at the Trailways and Greyhound bus terminals. In mid-March, four African Americans scored a victory when they were served at the Greyhound terminal. But as they tried to eat, whites physically assaulted them. Moreover, two bombs were found at the terminal the next day.

As in Montgomery in 1956, African Americans boycotted downtown Nashville stores in the winter and spring of 1960. "Don't Buy Downtown" was the slogan. Because many white people had moved to the suburbs, downtown storeowners had relied on black clientele. Very few African Americans violated the boycott. Even whites stayed away. Some whites avoided downtown because they feared the disturbances caused by the sit-ins, while other whites did so to support the civil rights cause. The boycott became so successful that a storeowner griped: "You could roll a bowling ball down Church Street and not hit anybody these days."

On March 3, Nashville mayor Ben West appointed a biracial committee to address the issues. On April 5, the committee recommended that Nashville's lunch counters be divided into white and black sections. The NCLC rejected the proposal, claiming correctly that it was just another form of segregation.

On April 19, before dawn, a bomb exploded, destroying the home of Z. Alexander Looby—the attorney who had represented the sit-in demonstrators. News of the incident spread quickly, and around noon activists began a protest march at Tennessee A&I College (now Tennessee State University) at the edge of the city limits. They headed toward city hall, and as they marched others joined their ranks. College students, high school kids, and adults—their numbers reaching 2,500—marched toward the heart of downtown. For a while they sang, but then they became solemnly quiet.

Marcher C. T. Vivian remembered the expressions on the white downtown workers, who were outside on their lunch hour. "[T]hey simply stood against the wall, just looking. There was a fear there, there was an awe there. They knew that this was not to be stopped, this was not to be played with or to be joked with."

Mayor West, who was more progressive than most of the other big-city mayors in the South, was angry about the pre-dawn bombing. By the time the marchers reached the steps of city hall, West was outside waiting to greet them. Diane Nash, who at age twenty-one had emerged as a leader of the Nashville movement, confronted the mayor while television cameras rolled.

She asked him if it was "wrong to discriminate against a person solely on the basis of his race or color." West said it was. She then asked him, "Mayor, do you recommend that the lunch counters be desegregated?" "Yes," he declared, and the crowd erupted in applause.

West's declaration was a pivotal point in the civil rights movement. A white mayor of a segregated southern city had stated that he was *against* segregation—and on television, no less. From that point on, the tide turned in Nashville. The next day, the local newspapers reported the mayor's desire to desegregate the lunch counters. Also that day,

Martin Luther King Jr. delivered a speech in the city. "I did not come to Nashville to bring inspiration," he said, "but to gain inspiration from the great movement that has taken place in this community. . . . [S]egregation is on its death-bed now, and the only uncertain thing about it is the day it will be buried."

Over the next few weeks, protest leaders and local merchants participated in secret discussions. Finally, on May 10, six Nashville stores opened their lunch counters to African Americans for the first time. As part of the agreement, they did so without fanfare. It would take more efforts to fully integrate Nashville. Protesters would stage "sleep-ins" in hotel lobbies and "stand-ins" in the city's movie theaters. However, the lunch counter successes had been a major triumph for the civil rights movement in Nashville—and the country as a whole.

In Greensboro, the sit-in movement remained on hiatus. After calling off the daily sit-ins following the early-February bomb threat, the Students Executive Committee for Justice tried to negotiate a desegregation settlement. Mayor George Roach put together the Mayor's Advisory Committee on Community Relations, headed by white businessman Edward Zane—an opponent of segregation.

In late February, Zane's committee mailed more than 5,000 letters to local citizens asking for their opinions about segregation. The committee received more than 2,000 responses, with 73 percent saying that they favored equality of service. Nevertheless, the committee was unable to secure integration. So, around April 1, demonstrations in Greensboro resumed. On April 21, forty-five protesters held a sit-in at the Kress store and refused to leave. Police arrived and arrested them. The black adults of Greensboro supported the student protesters by boycotting downtown businesses—a mass protest that lasted well into the summer.

In addition to Greensboro and Nashville, tremendous civil rights activity was occurring throughout the South. Beginning with a Kress sit-in on February 25, 1960, college students in Orangeburg, South Carolina, held sit-ins and carried picket signs for three weeks. On a frigid day on March 15, students Tom Gaither (Claflin College) and Chuck McDew (South Carolina State) led a march of one thousand students to downtown Orangeburg. Though their march was peaceful, police broke up the demonstration with clubs and tear gas while firefighters blasted them with their hoses. Three hundred were arrested.

In Montgomery, Alabama, hundreds of African Americans protested segregation at the former Confederate capitol building (on March 1) and the Alabama state capitol building (March 6). Across the South, successes were offset by backlash. On March 16, San Antonio, Texas, desegregated its lunch counters. But two weeks later, firefighters in Marshall, Texas, turned their hoses on sit-in demonstrators.

In Baltimore, Maryland, college students staged sit-ins and pickets at lunch counters, restaurants, and a movie theater. Reported Baltimore's newspaper, the *Sun,* "Two persons were arrested late yesterday afternoon in the four day-old anti-segregation demonstration at Hecht's Northwood restaurant and the restaurant closed for the day soon afterwards." Protesters in Baltimore toted signs that declared, "We'll Walk, Walk, Walk, Walk, Walk;" "We Want Equality;" and "We Will Never Stop Until You End Segregation."

By the end of March, an estimated eighty sit-ins had taken place, from as far north as Xenia, Ohio, to as far south as Sarasota, Florida. The most contentious battleground may have been in Baton Rouge, Louisiana. Anticipating sit-ins in their state, the all-white Louisiana State Board of Education promised stern disciplinary action against any Louisiana student who took part in a sit-in. The president of Southern University, (SU) an all-black public school in Baton Rouge, promised expulsion for any SU student who participated.

On March 28-29, sixteen SU students were arrested for holding sit-ins at the Kress lunch counter and the Greyhound bus terminal. The Kress group was charged with disturbing the peace, and their bail was set at the alarmingly high sum of $1,500. In protest, SU student Major Johns led a 3,500-student march to the state capitol on March 30. Johns and the sixteen sit-in activists were not only expelled from the university, but they were banned from all public schools in Louisiana.

In response, SU students banned together, calling for a strike of classes until the seventeen students were reinstated. Soon, hundreds of students left the school for good—some because their parents feared for their safety, and others out of protest. Eventually, the U.S. Supreme Court would overturn the convictions of the sixteen who were arrested.

Ella Baker of the SCLC wanted to bring order to the sit-in movement. So on Easter weekend, 1960, she sponsored a meeting of sit-in students at Shaw University in Raleigh, North Carolina. The meeting, called "Sacrifice for Dignity," attracted scores of students from twelve states. The black ministers of the SCLC expected to mentor the eager activists, but it didn't turn out that way. Baker encouraged the students to take control of their own destiny.

That weekend, the young activists formed the Student Nonviolent Coordinating Committee (SNCC; pronounced "snick"). It was not an arm of the SCLC or the NAACP but was instead its own independent organization. Diane Nash and John Lewis were among the civil rights activists who emerged as leaders. SNCC, which aimed to organize the many southern sit-ins, would become a major player in civil rights causes.

As 1960 progressed, activists staged civil rights protests in all sorts of segregated places. They held kneel-ins in whites-only churches, swim-ins at public pools, read-ins at libraries, and wade-ins at public beaches. On April 24, a riot erupted in Biloxi, Mississippi, after several dozen African Americans attempted to desegregate the whites-only beach. Ten people, including two whites, were wounded by gunshots.

Back in Greensboro, the months-long boycott was hurting downtown businesses. Finally, the storeowners caved in. On July 25, Woolworth's, Kress, and Meyer's Cafeteria all agreed to desegregate. Over the next week, several hundred African Americans celebrated their new freedom by eating and drinking at the infamous counters.

On May 6, President Dwight Eisenhower signed the Civil Rights Act of 1960. The law called for federal inspection of local voter registration polls, and it introduced penalties for anyone who obstructed someone's attempt to vote or register to vote. Eighteen southern Democrats had tried to prevent the bill from passing by staging their own sort of sit-in: a 125-hour filibuster—the longest in history. They needn't have worried so much. Despite the new federal legislation, southern whites would still find ways to keep African Americans from the polls.

In New Orleans, Louisiana, racial tensions were as heated as those across the state in Biloxi. In 1960, segregation gripped the city. On the famed Canal Street, lunch counters and restrooms were segregated. Even on Dryades Street, where the shoppers were virtually all black, storeowners hired only white employees (except janitors). In April 1960, the protests began. The Consumers' League of Greater New Orleans launched a long-lasting boycott of Dryades stores. It worked all too well, as many stores closed or moved to the suburbs.

On September 9, CORE held a sit-in at the Woolworth's on Canal Street. The protesters were arrested, and Oretha Castle (a CORE leader) was fired from her job at the Hotel Dieu Hospital. She recalled: "The good nun gave me my paycheck and said, 'Take it, and get out of here, and don't ever come back.'" When CORE and NAACP Youth Council members picketed stores, whites beat them and threw hot coffee and acid at them.

Picketing, sit-ins, boycotts, and arrests would continue in New Orleans for years, as the city would be a "tough nut to crack" for civil rights activists. At one rally, a white woman hoisted a sign that insisted, "Integration Is a Mortal Sin."

A student being carried out in the chair she was sitting in to protest segregation in New Orleans, Louisiana. *(Courtesy of AP Images)*

On August 27, a sit-in demonstration in Jacksonville, Florida, turned violent, resulting in numerous injuries. But just up the highway in racially moderate Savannah, Georgia, cooler heads prevailed. From March 1960 to October 1961, local activists staged peaceful boycotts and protests. Besides lunch counters, they targeted numerous other segregated facilities. The movement worked. By 1961, the city agreed to hire black bus drivers and to desegregate buses, parks, swimming pools, and restaurants.

By the fall of 1960, the dreams of the Greensboro Four and millions of African Americans were coming to fruition. On October 17, the Woolworth, Kress, Grant, and McCrory-McClellan stores made a joint announcement. They stated that lunch counters had been integrated in 112 southern cities—with many occurring in the previous eight months. A spokesman said the four companies were "conscious of a great social change occurring in the United States which has been dramatized by the students' sit-in movement."

In late October, the sit-ins landed Martin Luther King Jr. in the biggest predicament of his life. It all started back in March, when black university students in Atlanta formed the Committee on Appeal for Human Rights (COAHR). "Today's youth will not sit by submissively, while being denied all the rights, privileges, and joys of life," they declared. For months, sit-ins, boycotts, picketing, and arrests occurred in Atlanta.

In October, King joined young protesters in a sit-in at an Atlanta department lunch counter. Arrested and hauled off to jail, he and others refused to post bail. It was part of a "jail, no bail" tactic that was becoming common during the early 1960s. Activists felt they could gain more attention to their cause if they refused to pay bail and instead spent days behind bars.

The sit-in charges were dropped against King, but he was held for violating probation (he had been arrested for a minor driving violation). Showing his hostility toward the upstart civil rights leader, the judge sentenced King to four months of incarceration. It got worse from there. Late one night, King was secretly transferred to Reidsville State Penitentiary, where many African Americans worked on horrific chain gangs and others had mysteriously died. Fortunately, King was quickly released on bond thanks to the pleas of his wife, Coretta, and the string-pulling of Washington attorney Robert F. Kennedy.

Martin Luther King Jr., accompanied by Lonnie King (left) and an unidentified woman, walks by a segregation protester following his October 9, 1960, arrest in Atlanta. To the left and rear of King is his arresting officer, Atlanta Police Captain R. E. Little. *(Courtesy of AP Images)*

From February 1 to the end of 1960, the civil rights movement underwent profound changes. The cautious leadership of the NAACP and SCLC gave way to a confrontational mass movement of determined young people. These courageous activists would continue to stage sit-ins (and wade-ins, read-ins, and so on) in 1961 and beyond. In September 1961, the Southern Regional Council reported that some 70,000 people—in one hundred cities in twenty states—had been involved in sit-ins. The council stated that there had been 3,600 arrests, 187 students expelled from colleges and universities, and fifty-eight faculty members fired from their jobs. Moreover, the movement had succeeded in integrating one or more eating facilities in 108 cities.

Up through the mid-1960s, protesters staged "ins" throughout the South. But in June 1964, alarming events occurred in St. Augustine, Florida. It started when King, Ralph Abernathy, and others were arrested for protesting segregation at the Monson Motor Lodge. On June 18, Abernathy and fellow activists returned to stage a wade-in in the lodge's outdoor pool. "You can't do that. Get out!" ordered motel manager James Brock. They didn't move, so Brock came back with a bucket of hydrochloric acid. "Okay," he said, "this is acid. Acid! If you don't get out, I'll pour it in the water." And he did.

A week later, protesters held a wade-in at a St. Augustine beach. Their action provoked Klansmen and lawmen, who chased them into the "segregated" ocean and beat them with fists and clubs.

Four years earlier, on November 8, 1960, a new era dawned when John F. Kennedy (Robert's older brother) won the presidential election. Over the previous eight years, President Dwight Eisenhower had displayed only mild support for civil

Civil rights activists attempting to swim at a "whites only" beach in St. Augustine, Florida, are beaten and chased by violent segregationists. *(Courtesy of Rolls Press/Popperfoto/Getty Images)*

rights issues. President Kennedy would not initially be progressive on such matters, but events would develop in 1961 that would drag him into the civil rights fray and compel him and his brother to take action. Those events would forever be known as the Freedom Rides.

five

Prelude to the Freedom Rides

The story of the Freedom Rides began when an African American woman refused to give up her seat to a white person on a crowded bus. And her name was *not* Rosa Parks.

In 1944, Irene Morgan was a twenty-seven-year-old mother of two who worked in a factory that made bombers for the military. That July, after traveling to Virginia, she returned to her home in Baltimore aboard a Greyhound bus. When the bus became crowded, the driver told her to stand so that a white person could take her seat. After Morgan refused the command, the driver summoned the police.

"[The sheriff deputy] put his hand on me to arrest me, so I took my foot and kicked him," she recalled. Morgan reportedly kicked the deputy in the groin. "He was blue and purple and turned all colors," she said. "I started to bite him, but he looked dirty, so I couldn't bite him. So all I could do was claw and tear his clothes."

Morgan paid a $100 fine for resisting arrest, but she refused to pay her other ($10) fine—for violating a Virginia law that required segregated seating on public transportation. The Virginia courts ruled against her, but NAACP attorneys took the case to the U.S. Supreme Court. In *Morgan* v. *Virginia,* the court ruled in her favor. Although the court did not declare that segregated bus travel *within* a state was unconstitutional, it did rule that segregated seating in *interstate* travel

A 2000 photo of Irene Morgan *(Courtesy of AP Images/Newport News Daily Press, Kyndell Harkness)*

(that is, a bus that traveled from one state to another) violated the Constitution. (On November 25, 1955, the Interstate Commerce Commission would ban segregation in interstate bus and rail travel.)

This case caught the attention of the Congress of Racial Equality (CORE). An offshoot of the pacifist group Fellowship of Reconciliation, CORE had been founded in 1942 in Chicago. CORE leaders, such as James Farmer and Bayard Rustin, were intellectuals who lived on the fringe of society. Believers in the teachings of Gandhi and Henry David Thoreau, they were committed to fighting racial injustice through nonviolent protest.

In early 1947, CORE members announced that they would test the results of the *Morgan* v. *Virginia* decision. Sixteen

Above: James Farmer (*Courtesy of AP Images*)
Right: Bayard Rustin (*Library of Congress*)

members, eight white and eight black, would embark on the Journey of Reconciliation. They knew that Southerners had ignored the *Morgan* ruling, and they wanted to force the issue. If they were arrested, then attorneys and the media could bring attention to the injustice.

Leading NAACP attorney Thurgood Marshall strongly opposed the Journey of Reconciliation. A patient, sensible man, he believed that the best way to dismantle segregation was in the courts. He warned that a "disobedience movement on the part of Negroes and their white allies, if employed in the South, would result in wholesale slaughter with no good achieved." Nevertheless, the CORE members were determined to ride. The NAACP offered the services of their southern attorneys, which they undoubtedly would need.

The Journey of Reconciliation began on April 9, 1947, six days before Jackie Robinson broke Major League Baseball's

Members of the Journey of Reconciliation in 1947. Left to right: Worth Randle, Wallace Nelson, Ernest Bromley, James Peck, Igal Roodenko, Bayard Rustin, Joseph Felmet, George Houser, and Andrew Johnson.

color barrier. Besides Farmer and Rustin, who were black, Journey leaders included white pacifists George Houser and James Peck. Boarding Greyhound and Trailways buses, as well as trains, the travelers journeyed through Virginia, North Carolina, Tennessee, and Kentucky. Noticeably, they avoided the Deep South states, where resistance to integregation was especially vehement.

On the buses, some white CORE riders sat in the back and some black riders sat in the front, thus violating regional customs. Other blacks and whites sat side by side. At their many stops during the two-week journey, they spoke to church congregations and NAACP groups. Some sang a song that Rustin and Houser had penned:

You don't have to ride Jim Crow!
You don't have to ride Jim Crow,

On June the Third the high court said
When you ride interstate, Jim Crow is dead,
You don't have to ride Jim Crow . . .
Go quiet-like if you face arrest,
NAACP will make a test,
You don't have to ride Jim Crow!

Despite avoiding the Deep South states, the travelers met fierce resistance. They not only were arrested several times for violating segregation laws, but they were threatened and physically attacked. In Chapel Hill, North Carolina, a white cab driver punched Peck in the head for "coming down here to stir up the niggers."

On May 20, four of the riders appeared in a Chapel Hill court to await sentencing for an earlier arrest. Judge Henry Whitfield, a hard-line segregationist, sentenced African Americans Rustin and Andrew Johnson to thirty days on a chain gang. The judge delivered even harsher sentences to two of the white riders. He told Igal Roodenko and Joseph Felmet, "It's about time you Jews from New York learned that you can't come down her bringing your niggers with you to upset the customs of the South. Just to teach you a lesson, I gave your black boys thirty days, and I give you ninety."

Unlike Jackie Robinson's debut, the Journey of Reconciliation received little national attention in 1947 and is rarely discussed in history classes. But its impact was significant. In their talks at churches and college campuses, the activists enlightened and inspired hundreds of African Americans. Their story appeared in black newspapers, sparking hope that integration was coming.

Rustin's article, "Twenty-two Days on a Chain Gang," exposed brutal conditions in North Carolina's prisons, which led to prison reform in that state. Moreover, some of the Journey's participants, including Peck, organized the 1961 Freedom Rides. In fact, the two events are so intertwined that the Journey of Reconciliation is often called "the original Freedom Ride."

Ollie Stewart of the *Baltimore Afro-American* summed it up: "The Journey of Reconciliation, with whites and colored traveling and sleeping and eating together, to my way of thinking, made the solution of segregation seem far simpler than it ever had before. I heard one man refer to the group as pioneers. I think he had something there. They wrote a new page in the history of America."

six

Freedom Rides

J ames Farmer Sr. was believed to be the first black resident of Texas ever to earn a doctorate degree. But no matter his achievements and status, he could not shield his son, James Jr., from the evils of racism.

As a small child in Holly Springs, Mississippi, James Jr. asked his mother for a soft drink at a local drugstore. Despite sweltering heat, she told him that he'd have to wait until they got home. James pointed out that other children—white kids—were buying soda; why couldn't he have one? When they got home, his mother explained the awful truth. "Until then, I had not realized that I was colored . . ." Farmer said. "My mother fell across the bed and cried."

Experiencing more humiliating episodes while growing up, Farmer devoted his life to fighting segregation. He helped found CORE in 1942 and contributed to numerous civil rights causes up to the 1960s. On February 1, 1961—the first anniversary of the initial Greensboro sit-in—he started his first day as CORE's national director.

That morning, Farmer went to his new office and perused a stack of letters. Some of them included inquiries about the *Boynton* v. *Virginia* case, which the U.S. Supreme Court had decided on December 5, 1960. Undoubtedly, the case reminded him of *Morgan* v. *Virginia,* the 1946 decision that had outlawed segregated seating in interstate travel.

Back in 1958, Howard University law student Bruce Boynton rode a Trailways bus from Washington, D.C., to his home in Montgomery, Alabama. During a stop at the Trailways bus terminal in Richmond, Virginia, Boynton entered the terminal's restaurant, which was segregated. Sitting in the white section, he ordered a sandwich and tea. When an employee asked him to move to the black section, Boynton refused. He said that as an interstate passenger, he was protected by federal anti-segregation laws. Local officials didn't see it that way. Police arrested Boynton, charged him with trespassing, and fined him $10.

The case went all the way to the Supreme Court. On December 5, 1960, the court decided seven to two in favor of Boynton. Justice Hugo Black wrote:

> Interstate passengers have to eat, and they have a right to expect that this essential transportation food service . . . would be rendered without discrimination prohibited by the Interstate Commerce Act. We are not holding that every time a bus stops at a wholly independent roadside restaurant the act applies . . . [but] where circumstances show that the terminal and restaurant operate as an integral part of the bus carrier's transportation service . . . an interstate passenger need not inquire into documents of title or contractual agreements in order to determine whether he has a right to be served without discrimination.

So, fourteen years after ruling that interstate modes of transportation (buses and trains) should be integrated, the Supreme Court ruled that interstate facilities, such as bus terminal restaurants, should be integrated as well. Of course, what *should* be done was much different than the reality. In terminals throughout the South, "WHITES ONLY" signs still greeted those who stepped off the buses.

Later in his first day as CORE president, Farmer discussed the Boynton issue with his staff. Gordon Carey mentioned that he and Tom Gaither had discussed a sequel to the Journey of Reconciliation. They had given it a catchier name: Freedom Ride. Envisioning something similar to Gandhi's "March to the Sea," Carey and Gathier offered the idea of bus rides from Washington, D.C., to New Orleans.

A police officer stands beside a "white waiting room" sign at a Greyhound bus station in 1961. *(Courtesy of AP Images)*

Such rides would be more dangerous than the Journey of Reconciliation because activists would journey into the Deep South, where Ku Klux Klansmen loomed. But Farmer supported the idea, saying CORE wanted to put "the movement on wheels . . . to cut across state lines and establish the position that we were entitled to act any place in the country, no matter where we hung our hat and called home, because it was our country."

The CORE leaders laid their plans. On May 4, thirteen riders—seven black and six white—would leave Washington. One interracial group would travel on a Trailways bus and the other on a Greyhound. They would head south through Virginia, the Carolinas, Georgia, Alabama, and Mississippi and meet for a rally in New Orleans. They planned to arrive on May 17, the seventh anniversary of the *Brown* v. *Board of Education* decision (in which the Supreme Court ruled that segregated public schools were unconstitutional).

CORE leaders chose eleven riders from their organization and two from SNCC. They chose men and women who had clean records and reputations. Some of the riders were college students, including John Lewis of SNCC and Howard University student Hank Thomas, a sit-in veteran. Most were middle-age, including white Journey of Reconciliation participant James Peck. Dr. Walter Bergman, a sixty-one-year-old professor from Michigan, rode too—as did his wife, Frances.

According to CORE's plan, white riders would sit in the back of the buses and black riders would sit in the front. Though such seating violated laws in many parts of the South, the U.S. Supreme Court had deemed it acceptable. When ordered to move out of their sections, the riders would refuse, citing the Supreme Court rulings. They would do the same thing at the bus terminals. Blacks would use the white restrooms and vice versa.

Farmer said, "We felt that we could then count upon the racists of the South to create a crisis." In other words, should southern whites attack the Freedom Riders, it would make front-page headlines throughout the country. Most of the country would be appalled, and non-Southern politicians would seek justice. Desegregation would become a top priority in Washington, and the U.S. government would respond by enforcing federal law in the South. At least, that was CORE's ideal scenario.

Prior to the rides, Farmer sent heads-up letters to President John F. Kennedy, Attorney General Robert Kennedy, FBI Director J. Edgar Hoover, the chairman of the Interstate Commerce Commission, and the presidents of Trailways Corporation and Greyhound Corporation. No one responded to his letters. The Freedom Riders were on their own.

The riders expected to be attacked, possibly even severely. During their week of training, they learned (among other things) how to protect their faces and vital organs if they were beaten. Of course, they could do little to protect themselves from gunshots and dynamite. Some of the riders wrote letters to family members to be delivered if they were killed.

Before departure, the Freedom Riders ate together at a Chinese restaurant in Washington, a last night of relaxation and togetherness before the challenges they were about to face. On May 4, they departed on two buses, a Trailways and a Greyhound. Over the first week, they encountered only a few skirmishes. In Charlotte, North Carolina, one of the riders was arrested for trying to get a haircut and shoe-shine at a white barbershop. In Rock Hill, South Carolina, whites beat up Lewis and Al Bigelow, a white retired naval

CORE members look at a map prior to embarking on a Freedom Ride in 1961. *From left:* Edward Blankenheim, James Farmer, Genevieve Hughes, Rev. B. Elton Cox, and Hank Thomas. *(Courtesy of AP Images)*

officer. The two refused to press charges, and the rides continued.

Surprisingly, the riders were served with courtesy at segregated lunch counters in Augusta, Georgia, which would witness desegregation protests the following year. On May 13, they received a hero's welcome in Atlanta. Students and sit-in veterans cheered their arrival, and Martin Luther King Jr. dined with them at a nice black-owned restaurant that evening. Atlanta, the "City Too Busy to Hate," was large and progressive. King, though, worried about the Freedom Riders as they prepared to head further south. "You will never make it through Alabama," he told a journalist traveling with the riders.

On the morning of May 14, all the riders except Farmer—who left the Freedom Ride to attend his father's funeral—boarded the Trailways and Greyhound buses. They knew that grave danger lay ahead. They had talked on the phone with black reverend Fred Shuttlesworth, who said that Ku Klux Klansmen

John Lewis, national chairman of SNCC (*Courtesy of AP Images*)

were waiting for them. Between Atlanta and Birmingham, they were scheduled to stop only once, in Anniston, Alabama. It was there that the violence began.

Of the two buses, the Greyhound left Atlanta first, at 11 a.m. On board were driver O. T. Jones, seven Freedom Riders, two journalists, two regular passengers, the manager of the Atlanta Greyhound station, and (unbeknownst to the Freedom Riders) two undercover agents of the Alabama Highway Patrol. One of them, Eli Cowling, carried a hidden microphone.

As their bus neared Anniston, a highly segregated town that was 30 percent black, another Greyhound bus driver told them to pull over. That driver told Jones that a large, angry crowd had gathered in Anniston, and that the bus terminal had been closed. Joe Perkins, leader of this Freedom Ride group, urged Jones to continue to Anniston. When they arrived at 1 p.m., the station was closed and the area was apparently empty. Then, seemingly out of nowhere, several dozen whites raced toward the bus. They carried metal pipes, chains, and clubs and screamed at the Freedom Riders.

Some called the riders "dirty Communists;" for decades, southern whites had claimed that civil rights activists from the North had ties to Communist Russia. The activists' ultimate goal, some Southerners claimed, was not civil rights for African Americans but a Communist revolution in America. Communists did have some influence on civil rights activists prior to World War II, but they were a non-factor afterward.

Nevertheless, the whites of Anniston viewed the Freedom Riders as outside agitators who were out to destroy the southern way of life. Roger Couch, an eighteen-year-old Klansman, lay in front of the bus to prevent it from driving off. The two patrolmen on the bus, Cowling and Harry Sims, leaned on the front door's lever to prevent anyone from entering the vehicle. The mob took its rage out on the bus. They banged the metal, slashed the tires, and smashed windows (one person broke a pane with a rock; another with brass knuckles). One man pulled out his pistol and stared at Freedom Rider Genevieve Hughes for several minutes.

The siege lasted for nearly twenty minutes before Anniston police finally arrived (even though they had been warned ahead of time of the inevitable confrontation). The police escorted the bus to the edge of the city, then turned back. Meanwhile, several dozen cars and trucks followed the bus. After the police disappeared, two cars pulled in front of the bus and forced it to slow down. Six miles out of Anniston, Jones pulled over due to two flat tires. He and another man ran to a grocery store to call local mechanics. Meanwhile, the passengers were left to the mercy of the mob.

Patrolman Cowling pulled his gun out of the baggage department, but the attackers were undaunted. For at least twenty minutes, they rocked the bus, smashed another window, and urged the riders to come out. At one point, attacker Cecil "Goober" Llewallyn threw a bundle of flaming rags into the bus. The bundle exploded, filling the bus with thick, black smoke. With cries of "Burn them alive" and "Fry the goddamn niggers," some members of the mob leaned against the door so that the passengers couldn't escape. Only when the fuel tank exploded did the whites run from the bus. Cowling opened the door and most of the passengers ran out. The rest climbed out a window, falling hard to the ground.

As the bus burned, a white man asked Freedom Rider Hank Thomas if he was all right—then clubbed him in the head with

Freedom Riders sit on the roadside as their bus goes up in flames after being set on fire by an angry mob near Anniston, Alabama. *(Library of Congress)*

a baseball bat. The riders, having inhaled too much smoke, were in need of medical attention, but the mob persisted in their attacks and taunting. Only after a second explosion on the bus and pistol shots into the air by the highway patrolmen did the mob disperse. The passengers had trouble finding anyone who would transport them to the hospital, and even there Klansmen gathered, looking for another confrontation.

The superintendent of the hospital would not allow the Freedom Riders to stay overnight. Bravely, friends of Reverend Shuttlesworth drove from Birmingham to Anniston to rescue the activists. Surrounded by Klansmen, they led the riders into their cars and drove off.

About one hour after the Greyhound bus had arrived in Anniston on Sunday, the Trailways bus pulled into Anniston. Those passengers endured their own ordeal. Eight white men hijacked the bus, telling the driver to continue to Birmingham. The hijackers forcibly segregated the bus, dragging the African Americans to the rear seats. Those whites who objected were beaten with fists, clubs, and bottles. "We got clobbered on the head," recalled James Peck. "I didn't get it so bad, but [Walter] Bergman got it so bad that he later had a stroke and has been paralyzed ever since."

Peck "got it" when the bus arrived in Birmingham. As they exited the bus, the Freedom Riders were attacked by twenty Ku Klux Klansmen and other segregationists. The men, armed with metal pipes, beat and kicked Peck so badly that he lost consciousness, blood spilling from his head. The men attacked Bergman, who had lain unconscious on the bus, as well as black passengers, journalists, and bystanders.

Public Safety Commissioner Bull Connor had known that the Klansmen would greet and assault the Freedom Riders. However, he posted no officers at the station because, he said later, it was Mother's Day. In reality, the notorious segregationist had wanted to give the Klansmen fifteen minutes of beating time. When the police finally arrived, the mob dispersed.

The Freedom Riders had paid a heavy price, but they finally received the national attention they had been seeking. The next day, images of the burning bus and bloodied riders appeared in newspapers and on televi-

Bull Connor (*Courtesy of AP Images*)

sion. Peck, his face a mess, told reporters that he had received more than fifty stitches—but that he was determined to ride again. He needed to show, he said, "that nonviolence can prevail over violence."

The crisis was so big that President John F. Kennedy held an emergency meeting at 8:30 on Monday morning—while still in his pajamas. Kennedy had long expressed sympathy for the civil rights movement, but he had been reluctant to take strong action. The South was dominated by segregationist Democrats, and JFK did not want to alienate so many members of his own party.

Yet, Kennedy was also concerned about his country's image abroad. America was in the midst of its Cold War struggle with the Soviet Union. How could Kennedy preach freedom and democracy to the rest of the world when American citizens were denied such rights? JFK began to fully side with the movement. On May 15, he and Robert Kennedy decided to put federal marshals on call. They would go to Alabama if necessary. Meanwhile, Alabama governor John Patterson refused to take Robert Kennedy's phone call; his aides said he was out fishing.

After the violence, Trailways and Greyhound refused to transport the Freedom Riders. After all, the Greyhound bus had been completely destroyed. The riders pleaded with officials to continue, but the companies wouldn't budge. The activists gave up and flew out of Birmingham, but even at the airport they faced hostility from locals. The group flew to New Orleans, their original destination.

The Freedom Rides, however, were far from over. In fact, the CORE activists had inspired young activists to ride for freedom. In Nashville, sit-in veterans declared that they would go to Birmingham and continue the Freedom Rides—despite the extraordinary risks. Explained Nashville activist Diane Nash: "If the Freedom Riders had been stopped as a result of violence, I strongly felt that the future of the movement was going to be cut short. The impression would have been that whenever a movement starts, all [whites had to do was] attack it with massive violence and the blacks [would] stop."

Robert Kennedy agreed. The young attorney general, who in terms of civil rights was probably the most progressive cabinet member at that time, phoned Greyhound officials and the Birmingham police. Kennedy stressed to each the importance of upholding federal law. Greyhound agreed to drive the new Freedom Riders from Birmingham to Montgomery.

For the new wave of Freedom Rides, Nash selected ten students from the Central Committee of the Nashville Student Movement. Eight were black and two were white. On May 17, they traveled to Birmingham to revive the rides. When they got there, Bull Connor had them jailed, purportedly for their own safety. The activists responded by going on a hunger strike and singing "freedom songs." The next night, Connor released most of the Freedom Riders. He and his men drove them north to the Tennessee state line, where they dumped them off and told them to stay out of Alabama.

But back they came. A fellow Nashville student picked them up and drove them back to Birmingham. Other recruits joined them, bringing their number up to twenty-one. For eighteen hours, the Freedom Riders waited in a bus depot as government officials debated about what to do.

Robert Kennedy spoke on the phone to Governor Patterson, who agreed to meet with Justice Department aide John Seigenthaler—a Southerner, but one committed to civil rights. Seigenthaler flew to Montgomery, where he exchanged harsh words with the governor. According to Seigenthaler's account, Patterson said:

> The people of this country are so goddamned tired of the mamby-pamby that's in Washington, it's a disgrace. There's nobody in the whole country that's got the spine to stand up to the goddamned niggers except me. . . . I want you to know if the schools in Alabama are integrated, blood's going to flow in the streets, and you can take that message back to the president and you tell the attorney general that.

Seigenthaler stood his ground. He stated that the Freedom Riders were going to travel in Alabama, and if state officials refused to protect the riders, the federal government would bring in its own forces to protect them. Patterson responded that Alabama could capably police its state. Alabama public safety director Floyd Mann, who was in the meeting, promised to protect the riders from Birmingham to Montgomery. At that point, Mann said, the Montgomery police would take over.

Alabama governor John Patterson (seated, right) discusses the Freedom Rider situation with Deputy Attorney General Byron White (left). *(Courtesy of Joseph Scherschel/Time Life Pictures/Getty Images)*

Meanwhile, Robert Kennedy strongly urged Greyhound officials to transport the Freedom Riders, and they eventually agreed. On the morning of May 20, the riders boarded a Greyhound bound for Montgomery. Mann had made good on his promise, as state patrol cars lined the route to the state capital—but no further.

As the caravan reached the city limits, the patrol cars abandoned the bus, which pulled into the terminal all alone. The Montgomery police, who Mann had said would take over, were nowhere to be found. Instead, a mob of approximately three hundred—some armed with clubs and metal pipes—attacked the bus. When Jim Zwerg, a white Freedom Rider, exited the bus, a woman screamed, "Kill the nigger-lovin' son of a bitch." More than a dozen whites beat Zwerg, with one of them kicking in his front teeth.

"The mob turned from Zwerg to us," recalled Freedom Rider Ruby Doris Smith. "Someone yelled: 'They're about to get away!' Then they started beating everyone. I saw John Lewis beaten, blood coming out of his mouth. People were running from all over. Every one of the fellows was hit."

Reported witness William Orrick of the Justice Department: "People with no apparent connection to the trip were beaten, a boy's leg was broken, and another boy had inflammable liquid poured over him and set on fire." Black Freedom Rider William Barbee was beaten so badly that he would require a week's worth of hospital care. Siegenthaler was knocked unconscious.

The Montgomery police did arrive, but not until ten minutes after the rioting began. A larger "riot control" force

Jim Zwerg lies in a hospital bed after being severely beaten by a mob at a Montgomery bus station. *(Courtesy of AP Images/Horace Cort)*

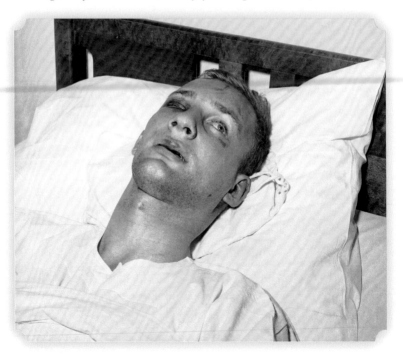

arrived an hour later, when the mob had swelled to a thousand people. Not all were bloodthirsty. Witnesses said that about two dozen people were responsible for the attacks, and Mann himself put a gun to the head of an attacker and told him to back off.

Nevertheless, Alabama had not protected the Freedom Riders—or even Siegenthaler, the representative of the president. Once again, the hate-filled violence dominated the news. Of the millions of Americans who witnessed the brutality in the media, many shared the same feelings: anger at the oppressors, sympathy for the oppressed (African Americans), and a determination to end segregation in the South. Newspapers from foreign countries reported on the events, putting the United States in a bad light and pressing Washington to shore up its "democracy."

Even an editorial writer for the *Atlanta Constitution,* the most prominent newspaper in the South, came down hard on segregationists. "Whatever one's views of the Freedom Riders, they have the right as citizens to ride a bus wherever it goes . . ." the editorial stated. "Alabama's shame, which is shared by the South, is also a serious blow to the security and prestige of the nation."

Robert Kennedy was furious at Alabama for allowing the Montgomery attacks to happen. In response, he sent six hundred federal marshals to Montgomery, many of whom guarded the hospital where Freedom Riders had been admitted. On Sunday, May 21, the marshals protected Reverend Ralph Abernathy's First Baptist Church in Montgomery. More than 1,200 people arrived that night to honor the Freedom Riders. Martin Luther King, Reverend Fred Shuttlesworth, and James Farmer were among the speakers.

Those in attendance were especially brave. Nighttime civil rights gatherings were always extra dangerous in the Deep South. Whites could commit crime in the anonymity of darkness, and tempers always seemed hotter late in the evening. Moreover, with tensions already burning in Montgomery, the mass gathering seemed all the more brazen.

Sure enough, an enormous mob enveloped the church. Some 3,000 whites cursed those inside, threw stones through the windows, and set cars on fire. Their presence turned into a siege, as they lingered until the wee hours of the morning while those inside were afraid to leave. At one point, the federal marshals tried to disperse the white crowd with tear gas, but it wafted into the church. Those inside coughed and feared for their lives.

At 3 a.m., King phoned Robert Kennedy, pleading for help. "If they don't get here immediately," King said, "we're going to have a bloody confrontation. Because they're at the door now." Kennedy responded by calling Governor Patterson, who gave the attorney general a tongue-lashing but agreed to declare martial law. Finally, state police and the Alabama National Guard escorted the people out of the church.

Later on Monday, President Kennedy expressed his frustrations. According to Robert Kennedy, "I think the president was fed up with John Patterson . . . he was [also] fed up with the Freedom Riders who went down there after [the bus bombing], when it didn't do any good to go down there." But to African Americans, the publicity that the Freedom Rides were creating was doing a world of good. This was revolutionary. After three hundred years of oppression, black Americans were shaping their destiny.

Despite Robert Kennedy's calls for a cooling-off period, more CORE and SNCC volunteers poured into Montgomery

An army truck transports people from the First Baptist Church of Montgomery following an overnight siege by a violent mob. *(Courtesy of Paul Schutzer/Time Life Pictures/Getty Images)*

to continue the Freedom Rides. On Monday and Tuesday, about twenty of them stayed at the home of Montgomery pharmacist Richard Harris, plotting their next move. All the while, a thousand National Guardsmen and reporters from across the country occupied the city.

At a press conference on Tuesday, King announced that the Freedom Riders would continue on to Mississippi. He himself would not go, largely because he was on probation and an arrest could lead to six months in jail. Filled with emotion, he said, "Freedom Riders must develop the quiet courage of dying for a cause. . . . I'm sure these students are willing to face death if necessary."

At 7:06 on Wednesday morning, twelve Freedom Riders—mostly from Nashville and led by James Lawson—left Montgomery, bound for Jackson, Mississippi. They had plenty of company. Sixteen reporters joined them on the bus, as did a dozen National Guard soldiers carrying bayoneted rifles. General Graham told the Freedom Riders, "I sincerely wish you all a safe journey"—a gesture of good faith that the riders noticeably appreciated. Dozens of reporters followed the Freedom Ride bus. So too did numerous highway patrol cars (sirens wailing) as well as helicopter escorts, the FBI, and U.S. Border Patrol airplanes.

Normally, the bus would stop several times during the 250-mile trip to Jackson. But on this day, it would travel nonstop. Earlier, Robert Kennedy and U.S. Senator James Eastland of

Freedom Rider David Dennis glances up at a National Guard soldier escorting the bus bound for Jackson, Mississippi. *(Courtesy of Paul Schutzer/Time Life Pictures/Getty Images)*

Mississippi had agreed how this ride would play out. Officials in Mississippi would ensure that the Freedom Riders would not be harmed, but once they arrived in Jackson they would be arrested for violating Mississippi segregation laws.

Like the southern politicians, Robert Kennedy was anxious to put the Freedom Rides to rest. His brother would soon travel to Europe for an immensely important summit with Soviet leader Nikita Khrushchev. How could President Kennedy hail American democracy while double rebellion (by segregationists and civil rights activists) was brewing back home?

Robert Kennedy thought the Wednesday episode would go smoothly, but then he heard that a second group of Freedom Riders had bought late-morning Greyhound tickets in Montgomery. The attorney general was irate, realizing that everything could get out of hand again. He responded by telling reporters that the fourteen men and women in the second group of riders had nothing to do with the Freedom Riders.

But this was every bit a Freedom Ride, and everyone knew it. One member of the group was Hank Thomas, who had been on the burning bus in Anniston. Days after that harrowing event, Thomas had said, "I was hit over the head with a club. Even now my chest hurts and I almost conk out every time I climb a few steps. But I'm ready to volunteer for another ride. Sure. Any time."

As the second bus was about to depart, a hostile crowd of 2,000 swarmed the Montgomery bus terminal, as did a horde of reporters. When the Freedom Riders entered the bus, so too did more National Guardsmen. CORE President James Farmer, after seeing a look of fear in the eyes of a nineteen-year-old female rider, joined the ride at the last minute.

Much to Robert Kennedy's relief, both buses arrived safely in Jackson, with no mobs awaiting them. When the

Police officers with dogs watch as a bus carrying Freedom Riders arrives in Jackson. The officers arrested those on board as soon as they arrived. *(Library of Congress)*

black riders entered the whites-only waiting room, police steered them to a paddy wagon. All twenty-seven Freedom Riders, from both buses, were arrested. On May 26, the riders went on trial for violating state law. They didn't stand a chance in the segregated courtroom. As attorney Jack Young spoke in defense of the riders, the judge turned his back on him. He then sentenced them to sixty days in the state penitentiary.

The Freedom Riders chose to stay in jail rather than post bail. Martyrs for their cause, they sought to prolong media attention. While King supported their courageous "jail no bail" tactic, Robert Kennedy did not, and the two argued about it over the phone. The Freedom Riders stayed in prison, but it turned into a lose-lose situation. They endured the harshness of prison life without helping their cause: after their arrest, the Freedom Rides were no longer a news story.

On May 25, President John Kennedy delivered a historic address to Congress. He announced his commitment to put a man on the moon, and he promoted a "freedom doctrine"— support for the freedom-seeking peoples of Asia, Latin America, Africa, and the Middle East. "They seek an end to injustice, tyranny, and exploitation," he declared. Ironically, the president did not mention the Freedom Riders or anything else about the civil rights movement.

A Freedom Rider is escorted out of a white waiting room in Jackson, Mississippi. *(Courtesy of William Lovelace/Express/Getty Images)*

But while Washington and the news media moved on to other issues, Freedom Rides continued. Members of CORE, SNCC, and the SCLC formed the Freedom Riders Coordinating Committee to continue the Rides. Over the summer, more than 430 Freedom Riders (a mix of black and white) participated in more than sixty Freedom Rides. Participants, who hailed from all regions of the country, included college and high school students; ministers, priests, and rabbis; doctors and nurses; and blue-collar workers and housewives. Norma Wagner, a blind activist, also rode.

The Freedom Rides started and/or ended in such cities as Montgomery, Atlanta, Nashville, Memphis, New Orleans, St. Louis, Washington, Tallahassee, St. Petersburg, Little Rock, Shreveport, Houston, and others. At least three hundred Freedom Riders went to Jackson, where they were all arrested and convicted. Their strategy was to fill the local jails. Once they did that, officials transferred them to Parchman Penitentiary.

Those who ran Parchman were notorious for their abuse of prisoners, and they certainly did not take kindly to Freedom Riders. Many of these demonstrators were treated like heinous criminals. Their abuse included placement on "death row," denial of exercise and mail, and the issuance of only underwear. When the Freedom Riders refused demands to stop singing freedom songs, guards took away their mattresses and removed the screens on their windows. After mosquitoes swarmed into the cells, prisoners were sprayed with DDT, a toxic, dangerous chemical.

Freedom Riders who were sent to jails (as opposed to Parchman) reported their own horror stories. Ralph Fertig, a white man, attempted a Montgomery-to-Jackson Freedom Ride. Early in the ride, he yielded his seat to a black woman, which angered white passengers. As the bus pulled into Selma, Alabama, Sheriff Jim Clark grabbed Fertig by the collar, and had him sent to jail. Ku Klux Klansmen came to the jail, wanting to stir up the southern white prisoners, hoping they would take their wrath out on the "agitator."

"He's a gah-damned, nigger-loving Freedom Rider, boys," Fertig recalled one saying, "wants to put black bucks upside yer wives!" Said another: "We've got a necktie party waitin' fer him outside. If he don't leave here feet first, he ain't leavin' town no other way."

The white prisoners responded by beating and whipping Fertig. They "crushed my every rib until only the proud awareness that I would die for my most passionately held ideals kept me from crying out." The attackers stopped beating Fertig only when a black porter arrived to mop the floors. The porter understood this, so he kept on mopping—and mopping and mopping. Fertig would be forever grateful to the stranger who tried to save his life.

After thirty-six hours, lawyers for the movement (including Rosa Parks' attorney, Fred Gray) led Fertig out of jail. Outside, two crowds—one white and one black—looked on. Fertig, tears streaming, addressed the African Americans. "How do you keep from hating white folks?" he asked.

During the 1961 Freedom Rides, activists targeted other establishments. Blacks and whites tried to desegregate lunch counters, restaurants, and hotels. In essence, they were continuing the sit-in movement that had begun a year earlier.

Though these Freedom Riders no longer commanded the national spotlight, their persistence and large numbers had a cumulative effect. Adhering to Martin Luther King Jr.'s philosophy, their "capacity to suffer" wore down the opposition. Some whites in the South were tired of fighting these battles.

And as the Freedom Rides continued, Americans of all races and creeds railed against southern segregation.

Eventually, the continuous Freedom Rides prompted President Kennedy to address the issue. "In my judgment," he said to the press on July 19, "there's no question of the legal rights of the freedom travelers, Freedom Riders, to move in interstate commerce. And those rights, whether we agree with those who travel, whether we agree with the purpose for which they travel, those rights stand, providing they are exercised in a peaceful way."

Freedom Riders eating at a bus station lunch counter during their trip across the South. *(Courtesy of AP Images)*

In reaction to the months-long Freedom Rides, Robert Kennedy asked the Interstate Commerce Commission (ICC) to issue a desegregation order. On September 22, the ICC banned segregation at interstate highway facilities. The order would go into effect on November 1, 1961. At most interstate bus and train terminals, "WHITE" and "COLORED" signs were removed from the doorways of waiting rooms, restrooms, and lunch counters. Some terminals still refused to remove such signs, but overall it was a great victory for the civil rights movement.

Pleased enough with the outcome, King turned his attention away from interstate travel and toward other areas of racial injustice. After November 1, only a handful of Freedom Rides took place over the rest of the year. The last, according to Freedom Ride historian Raymond Arsenault, occurred on December 10, when teenager Joan Browning rode to Albany, Georgia—the stage for the next civil rights showdown.

seven

A Lasting Impact

T he civil rights movements culminated in the 1960s with well-orchestrated campaigns in four specific areas: Albany, Georgia (1961-62); Birmingham, Alabama, (1963); Mississippi (Freedom Summer, 1964); and Selma, Alabama (1965). The battles and successes in these areas led directly to the passage of the 1964 Civil Rights Act and the 1965 Voting Rights Act—pieces of legislation that virtually ended Jim Crow segregation in the South. Yet these campaigns were not isolated events. In fact, they were directly linked to the sit-ins and Freedom Rides that had preceded them.

SNCC, which was founded in 1960 to coordinate the sit-ins, initiated a voter registration drive in and around Albany in August 1961. Shortly afterward, members tried to desegregate the area as well. Recalled SNCC field secretary Charles Sherrod, "Sometimes we'd walk down the streets and the little kids would call us Freedom Riders." On November 1, 1961, the day that the ICC ruling banning segregation at bus and train stations went into effect, nine students staged a sit-in at an Albany bus station.

SNCC, the NAACP, the SCLC (including Martin Luther King Jr.), and other organizations became involved in the Albany movement. Over the next nine months, they staged mass marches, boycotts of white stores, sit-ins, jail-ins, and Freedom Rides. Nearly five hundred protesters were arrested in the first two weeks, with many more arrests following. Albany's white establishment "won" the segregation battle

Protesters stand outside city hall in Albany, Georgia, during a movement to end segregation in the city.

due to their self-discipline—that is, refraining from attacking the activists. However, the civil rights leaders learned valuable lessons in Albany, which they would apply in later campaigns. Moreover, the Albany campaign may not have ever begun at all had its citizens not been emboldened by the sit-ins and Freedom Rides.

Throughout the early and mid-1960s, sit-ins and other "ins" occurred throughout the South. On March 16, four gutsy Howard University students staged a sit-in in Robert Kennedy's outer office. They wanted to talk to him about a person who was being unfairly incarcerated. In summer 1962, NAACP members picketed segregated hotels, motels, and restaurants in Atlanta. On August 19, 1962, hundreds of African Americans staged demonstrations in North Carolina at two Howard Johnson's restaurants and motor lodges. In February 1963, four hundred protesters were arrested at a whites-only movie theater in Baltimore, Maryland. Such uprisings were happening throughout the South. They were the essence of the civil rights movement.

When members of the SCLC (which had been established well before the sit-ins) ran the famous Birmingham campaign of 1963, they launched it with marches and sit-ins. Moreover, the spirit of the 1960 and 1961 activists inspired Birmingham's black citizenry to action. That city had been considered the most segregated in the South, but African Americans took to the streets by the hundreds. Police officers sicced their dogs on the demonstrators, onlookers hurled bottles and bricks, and fire fighters sprayed them with their hoses (with blasts strong enough to break ribs), but still they marched on.

By the summer of 1963, civil rights activists had won over much of America. On August 28, some quarter-million people—mostly black, but many white—converged on

A policeman uses a dog to attack a civil rights protester in Birmingham, Alabama. *(Courtesy of AP Images)*

Washington, D.C. That day, Martin Luther King Jr. delivered his "I Have a Dream" speech, one of the most famous and important orations in American history. King captured the spirit of the sit-ins and Freedom Rides when he declared, "This is no time to engage in the luxury of cooling off or to take the tranquilizing drug of gradualism. Now is the time to make real the promises of democracy."

And certainly every person who sat in or rode for freedom could hold their heads high when King intoned: "Some of you have come from areas where your quest for freedom left you battered by the storms of persecution and staggered by the winds of police brutality. You have been the veterans of creative suffering. Continue to work with the faith that unearned suffering is redemptive."

Martin Luther King Jr. delivers his "I Have a Dream" speech in Washington, D.C. *(Courtesy of Department of Defense)*

In addition to King, John Lewis of SNCC also spoke to the masses that day. Lewis had come of age as a sit-in participant and Freedom Rider, and on August 28 he addressed America. He captured the urgency of the young grassroots protesters when he declared, "We must say wake up America, wake up! For we cannot stop, and we will not and cannot be patient."

It is difficult to imagine the fate of the civil rights movement had the Greensboro Four not triggered the sit-in movement in 1960. What is known is that the years after the Montgomery bus boycott, 1957 to 1959, had been quiet. But 1960 to 1963—with the sit-ins, Freedom Rides, and subsequent Albany and Birmingham campaigns—were the most eventful civil rights years of all. In the fall of 1963, Gallup Poll respondents proclaimed that civil rights was the most important crisis facing the nation.

Deborah Rand, a college student in Minnesota in the early 1960s, was among those who had been awakened by the activists. "I have always felt that the people in the civil rights movement were the most courageous and inspiring Americans of my generation," she wrote. "I was in awe of the sheer beauty of the people who sat down at lunch counters, picketed stores, participated in Freedom Rides, got arrested demanding the right to vote, and demanded that the United States become a real democracy."

In 1964, under President Lyndon Johnson, Congress responded to the will of the people. No longer willing to yield to the objections of white Southerners, Congress passed the Civil Rights Act of 1964. This was the most important civil rights legislation of the century. The act banned discrimination in places of public accommodations; barred unequal voter registration requirements; gave the U.S. attorney general more power to file lawsuits in order to protect citizens against discrimination; required the elimination of discrimination in federally assisted programs; established the Equal Employment Opportunity Commission (EEOC); and authorized the commissioner of education to help communities desegregate schools.

The Civil Rights Act would prove effective at ending segregation in public facilities in the South. However, it did lack the enforcement power to end voting injustice in the South.

In 1964, a group of volunteers was determined to tackle voting and other forms of discrimination throughout the state of Mississippi. The status of African Americans in Mississippi was astonishingly poor. The state spent four times more money educating a white student than it did a black pupil. Only about 7 percent of African Americans finished high school, and the average salary of a black Mississippian was one-third of a white person's. Forty-five percent of the state's population was black, but to maintain supremacy whites employed various forms of intimidation to keep African Americans out of the voting booth. On the strength of such efforts, only 6.7 percent of Mississippi blacks were registered to vote, according to the 1960 census.

In June 1964, the Council of Federated Organizations (COFO) launched the Mississippi Summer Project—more commonly known as Freedom Summer. Their goal was to get as many of the state's African Americans to vote as possible. COFO was an umbrella organization comprised partly of SCLC, NAACP, and CORE volunteers. But most of the COFO volunteers were members of SNCC, the direct-action organization that had helped organize the sit-ins—and which had reenergized the Freedom Rides once the CORE rides had ended.

The COFO workers oversaw hundreds of volunteers— mostly white college students. COFO/SNCC was able to attract these white volunteers because of their own courageous acts earlier in the decade. SNCC activists, in the eyes of many college students, were genuine heroes.

Kay Michener explained why she signed up for Freedom Summer: "I saw a documentary on Channel 11 in Chicago about an integrated group who took a ferry ride near New Orleans and were all arrested," she wrote. "I was appalled. When I found out through SNCC that black people were systematically prevented from voting all through the South, I realized that democracy in the USA was not working and could not survive unless everyone was voting."

During Freedom Summer, COFO workers and the volunteers registered black Mississippians and taught reading and other subjects in Freedom Schools. White supremacists, who felt that their state had been invaded by agitators, responded by harassing, arresting, and attacking (in some cases fatally) the activists. But as with the sit-ins and Freedom Rides, the activists' efforts brought national attention to their cause. After the triple murder of Freedom Summer volunteers James Chaney, Andrew Goodman, and Michael Schwerner, millions of Americans agreed that something had to be done to end voting injustice.

In the early months of 1965, King and the SCLC led a movement to end voting discrimination in Selma, Alabama. SNCC members, most notably John Lewis, contributed too. By the hundreds, activists waited in voter-registration lines, marched for justice, and were carted off to jail. State troopers attacked marchers on "Bloody Sunday," but eventually protesters walked all the way from Selma to the state capital.

Greatly motivated by the events in Mississippi and Selma, Congress passed the Voting Rights Act of 1965. The act

The murder of Freedom Summer volunteers Michael Schwerner, James Chaney, and Andrew Goodman brought even further attention to the civil rights movement. *(Courtesy of AP Images)*

SCHWERNER   CHANEY   GOODMAN

banned biased literacy tests and other exclusionary screening devices used by registrars to keep African Americans from voting. The act also allowed federal workers to register black voters when necessary.

Due to the new legislation, the walls of disenfranchisement came tumbling down. From August 6, 1965—the day that the Voting Rights Act was signed—to August 25, federal registrars registered 27,385 African Americans in Mississippi, Alabama, and Louisiana. By late October, the number jumped to 110,000. From 1960 to 1968, the percentage of registered of African American voters in Mississippi soared from 6.7 percent to 59 percent.

Armed with the ballot, black citizens had a strong impact on elections. White candidates had to be much more moderate to get elected, and in many cases African Americans won elections in the South. In the 1970s, African Americans Maynard Jackson and Richard Arrington were elected mayor of Atlanta and Birmingham, respectively. By the late 1960s, "WHITES ONLY" signs had all but disappeared in the South. Less-obvious forms of discrimination would persist in America for decades (and persist to this day), but nonviolent activism had pretty much destroyed Jim Crow segregation in the South.

Today's teachers credit Martin Luther King Jr., Rosa Parks, and other icons for fueling the civil rights movement. But much of the credit should go to the thousands of sit-in activists for getting the ball rolling and to the hundreds of Freedom Riders for keeping the buses going. Moreover, the impact of these activists was felt well beyond the realm of black civil rights.

In workshops at the beginning of Freedom Summer, SNCC and CORE leaders taught nonviolent tactics to the volunteers—the white college students. These students absorbed these lessons and used them in subsequent protest movements. For example, on October 1, 1964, University of California-Berkeley graduate student Jack Weinberg was arrested for setting up a civil rights information table on campus. Berkeley students protested, triggering the Free Speech Movement (FSM). On December 2-3, FSM leaders staged a sit-in, resulting in the arrests of more than seven hundred demonstrators.

White FSM leader Mario Savio had been inspired by SNCC activists while volunteering for Freedom Summer. "Last summer I went to Mississippi to join the struggle there for civil rights," he said. "This fall I am engaged in another phase of the same struggle, this time in Berkeley."

The young participants of the civil rights movement also had an impact on the antiwar movement that emerged in the mid-1960s, when conflict raged in Vietnam. In 1961, Students for a Democratic Society (SDS) member Tom Hayden, a white University of Michigan student, was beaten in McComb, Mississippi. He was inquiring about the expulsion of two black high school students who had participated in a bus station sit-in. A civil rights activist himself, Hayden went on to become president of the SDS, which took a leading role in the antiwar movement.

On March 24, 1965, faculty and students at the University of Michigan staged a "teach-in." Its name derived from "sit-in," the teach-in was an open forum for discussion of the Vietnam War. Many teach-ins sprouted on campuses throughout the country that year, and on May 15, 1965, radio broadcasts linked 122 campuses in a nationwide teach-in. In 1969, the Vietnam Moratorium Committee planned a much greater national teach-in. On October 15 of that year, as many as 10 million people participated. They took the day off from work or school to discuss how to end the war. Student activism, modeled after civil rights activism, helped convince the rest of America that the war needed to end. In a national poll taken shortly after the great teach-in of 1969, 60 percent of Americans called the war a mistake.

The civil rights activists also inspired other movements. The women's rights movement, the gay rights movement, and the movement for the rights of disabled Americans all used sit-ins, marches, and voluntary arrests as tools of protest. Over the years, protesters would employ such tactics as bed-ins (for peace), work-ins (working without pay when employees' jobs were threatened), and die-ins (feigning death as a protest of war).

The sit-in protesters also influenced oppressed people in other countries. In 1967, activists founded the Northern Ireland Civil Rights Association (NICRA). Its leaders— Catholics who faced oppression from Protestants—made a conscious effort to follow the model of the American civil rights movement. They picketed, marched, and even staged sit-ins.

Blacks attempted similar tactics in South Africa during the 1960s, when whites severely oppressed them in a notorious system called apartheid. "[W]e lived through the experiences of the [American] civil rights movement," said Franklin Sonn of South Africa, who in 1995 became that country's ambassador to the United States. "When the time came, we took over the same methods as the sit-ins and civil disobedience."

Ironically, SNCC turned away from sit-ins and nonviolent protests. Emboldened by their successes, frustrated by continued discrimination and poverty, and sick of "turn the other cheek" nonviolence, SNCC leaders became much more assertive. Under the leadership of the vocal Stokely Carmichael, SNCC trumpeted "Black Power" and became the first civil rights group to denounce U.S. involvement in Vietnam.

In June and July 1967, black angst overflowed in Detroit, Michigan, and Newark, New Jersey. Race riots erupted in both cities, resulting in sixty-nine total deaths. On July 24, 1967, new SNCC National Chairman H. Rap Brown fueled the fires when he declared in Cambridge, Maryland, "If America don't come around, we're going to burn it down." After the speech, black citizens in Cambridge started to riot.

Stokely Carmichael *(Courtesy of AP Images)*

Hundreds of people damage property and loot stores during a race riot in Detroit on July 23, 1967. *(Courtesy of AP Images)*

The aggressive tone of such black groups as SNCC and the Black Panthers caused a strong backlash. Richard Nixon won the presidency in 1968 on a "law and order" platform, and white city-dwellers responded to the riots and black militancy by moving to the suburbs. This wasn't the only reason they moved to the suburbs, of course, but it was certainly a contributing factor. In the 1970s

H. Rap Brown *(Library of Congress)*

and '80s, "white flight" occurred in Detroit, Cleveland, Washington, and many other big cities. Since whites in general had the higher incomes, the cities lost precious tax revenue when they left. Cities became economically impoverished, leading to rundown neighborhoods, hopelessness, high crime, and the selling of illegal drugs. In some neighborhoods, black males were more likely to go to prison than to college.

In the early days of the civil rights movement, leaders of the NAACP, SCLC, CORE, and SNCC had warned about the inevitable backlash that would result from aggressive confrontations. Black Americans may have been right to demand immediate justice, but militancy as a *tactic,* they had preached, would not work. That is why the Greensboro

Four—despite the anger in their hearts—had walked into Woolworth's in their finest clothes, had requested their coffee and pie politely, and had waited like gentlemen for service. It was the *nonviolent* aspect of their protest that led to the extraordinary success of the sit-in movement.

Unlike Rosa Parks, whose defiance in Montgomery helped spark the modern civil rights movement, the Greensboro Four never became American icons. Ezell Blair Jr., the leader of the quartet, has lived a productive life. Now known as Jibreel Khazan, he is married with three children and works with developmentally disabled people in New Bedford, Massachusetts. Franklin McCain, also married with three kids, has enjoyed a fruitful career as a chemist and engineer.

Joseph McNeil, married with five children, was a captain in the Air Force and is a major general in the Air Force Reserves. He has worked as a computer salesman, stockbroker, and commercial banker. David Richmond, a business major at North Carolina A&T, worked various jobs and fathered two children. After lung cancer took his life at age forty-nine, A&T awarded him a posthumous honorary doctorate degree.

The citizens of Greensboro proudly honor the accomplishments of these four men. The International Civil Rights Center and Museum, located on the same street as the old Woolworth's in Greensboro, features the lunch counter where the Greensboro Four initially demanded service.

On February 2, 2001, North Carolina A&T paid tribute to the Greensboro Four with the unveiling of a monument that is named "February One." Featuring sculptures of the four men together, "February One" stands in front of the school's Dudley Memorial Building.

Ron McNeil, Joseph's son, was among those who honored the Greensboro Four that day. "Great people don't always know that what they are doing at the time will later be perceived as something great," Ron said. "They weren't great at the time, but they had courage."

Richmond's son, David, fought off tears as he stared at the sculpture of his late father. "He would like it," he managed to say, "like I do."

The "February One" monument on the campus of North Carolina A&T State University in Greensboro.

Timeline

1943
May 14: Congress of Racial Equality (CORE) stages first sit-in at Jack Spratt Coffee Shop in Chicago.

1946
June 3: In *Morgan* v. *Virginia,* U.S. Supreme Court rules segregation in interstate bus travel unconstitutional.

1947
April: CORE sends eight black and eight white riders on "Journey of Reconciliation."

1955
November 25: Interstate Commerce Commission bans segregation in interstate bus and rail travel.

December 1: Montgomery bus boycott begins.

1958
Summer: Members of NAACP Youth Councils hold successful sit-ins at lunch counters in Wichita, Kansas, and Oklahoma City, Oklahoma.

1959
Spring: CORE organizes nonviolent sit-ins in Miami.

1960

February 1: North Carolina A&T students Ezell Blair Jr., Joseph McNeil, David Richmond, and Franklin McCain stage sit-in at whites-only lunch counter in Woolworth's in Greensboro, North Carolina.

February 2-6: Hundreds of North Carolina A&T students, and others, return for more sit-ins at Greensboro lunch counters.

Early to mid-February: Sit-ins spread to cities in North Carolina and other states.

February 13-27: Hundreds of young people stage sit-ins in Nashville.

March 28-29: Students hold sit-ins at Southern **University** in Louisiana, resulting in expulsions, mass march, and student strike.

April 19: In Nashville, activists march on City Hall; Mayor Ben West says city's lunch counters should be desegregated.

March 15: In Atlanta, Committee on Appeal for Human Rights holds its first sit-in.

March 16: San Antonio, Texas, becomes first major southern city to integrate lunch counters.

April 15:	In Raleigh, North Carolina, college studen. establish Student Nonviolent Coordinating Committee (SNCC).
May 10:	Six Nashville stores open lunch counters to African Americans for first time.
July 25:	Lunch counters in Greensboro desegregate
September 9:	CORE holds sit-in at the Woolworth's in New Orleans.
December 5:	In *Boynton* v. *Virginia,* U.S. Supreme Court rules segregation in interstate bus terminal facilities unconstitutional.
1961 March 7:	In Atlanta, city officials agree to integrate lunch counters.
May 4:	Thirteen CORE-sponsored Freedom Riders board two buses in Washington, D.C bound for New Orleans.
May 14:	In Anniston, Alabama, a white mob attacks and firebombs one of two Freedom Ride buses; riders in other bus are badly beaten when they arrive in Birmingham.
May 17:	Students from Nashville arrive in Birmingham to continue Freedom Rides.

May 20:	New Freedom Riders leave Birmingham, are badly beaten in Montgomery.
May 21:	Mob of more than 1,200 people threatens African Americans inside First Baptist Church in Montgomery.
May 24:	Twenty-seven Freedom Riders are arrested when they arrive in Jackson, Mississippi.
September 22:	Prompted by Robert Kennedy, Interstate Commerce Commission bans segregation at interstate travel facilities.

1964

| July 2: | President Lyndon Johnson signs Civil Rights Act of 1964. |

1965

| August 6: | President Johnson signs Voting Rights Act of 1965, effectively ending black disenfranchisement. |

Sources

CHAPTER ONE: Sitting and Riding for Freedom

p. 11, "At the rate . . ." James Baldwin, *The Price of the Ticket: Collected Nonfiction, 1948-1985* (New York: Macmillan, 1985), 266.

p. 12, "I'd like a . . ." Albert L. Rozier Jr., "Students Hit Woolworth's for Lunch Service," *Register* (A&T Student Newspaper), February 5, 1960.

p. 12, "You are stupid . . ." Ibid.

p. 14, "Other side, nigger . . ." Raymond Arsenault, *Freedom Riders* (New York: Oxford University Press, 2006), 122.

p. 14, "I have a . . ." Ibid.

p. 14, "The next thing . . ." Ibid.

p. 14, "All right, boys . . ." Ibid.

CHAPTER TWO: Jim Crow Has to Go

p. 16, "Our seedy run-down . . ." Pauli Murray, *Proud Shoes: The Story of an American Family* (Beacon Press, 1999), 270.

p. 17, "I can still . . ." William M. Simons and Alvin L. Hall, *The Cooperstown Symposium on Baseball and American Culture* (Jefferson, N.C.: McFarland, 2001), 241.

p. 18, "that all persons . . ." "The Emancipation Proclamation," National Park Service, http://www.nps.gov/ncro/anti/emancipation.html.

p. 24, "I say segregation . . ." "The 1963 Inaugural Address of Governor George C. Wallace," Alabama Department of Archives and History, http://www.archives.state.al.us/govs_list/inauguralspeech.html.

p. 24, "If you succeed . . ." "Theodore G. Bilbo and the Decline of Public Racism, 1938-1947," *Democratic Underground*, http://www.democraticunderground.com/discuss/duboard.php?az=show_mesg&forum=132&topic_id=4097733&mesg_id=4097733.

p. 25, "ensure the political . . ." "Our Mission," NAACP, http://www.naacp.org/about/mission.

p. 26, "It's in your . . ." Tony Chapelle, "Adam Clayton Powell, Jr.," *Black Collegian Online*, http://www.black-collegian.com/african/adam.shtml.

p. 27, "You couldn't possibly . . ." Clayborne Carson, primary consultant, *Civil Rights Chronicle: The African-American Struggle for Freedom* (Lincolnwood, Ill.: Legacy Publishing, 2003), 145.

p. 28, "I told them . . ." "James Farmer: Civil Rights Pioneer Farmer Dies," Associated Press, http://www.angelarose.com/FamousDiabetics/Fam-Political.htm.

p. 29, "we deliberately chose . . ." Carla Eckels, "Kansas Sit-In Gets Its Due at Last," NPR, October 21, 2006, http://www.npr.org/templates/story/story.php?storyId=6355095.

p. 29, "She gave it . . ." Ibid.

p. 29, "He came to . . ." Ibid.

p. 31, "Six days of . . ." Jeff Goodwin and James M. Jasper, *The Social Movements Reader: Cases and Concepts* (Oxford, England: Blackwell Publishing, 2003), 231.

CHAPTER THREE: The Greensboro Sit-Ins

p. 33, "I had lived . . ." Carson, *Civil Rights Chronicle,* 179.

p. 36, "Fifteen seconds after . . ." Michele Norris, "The Woolworth Sit-In That Launched a Movement," February 1, 2008, NPR, http://www.npr.org/templates/story/story.php?storyId=18615556.

p. 36, "We advised the . . ." Winslow, "The Fight for Civil Rights: In their own words."

p. 36, "She said in . . ." Michele Norris, "The Woolworth Sit-In That Launched a Movement."

p. 36, "What I learned . . ." Ibid.

p. 36, "They can just . . ." Lisa Cozzens, "Sit-in," Watson. org, June 22, 1998, http://www.watson.org/~lisa/ blackhistory/civilrights-55-65/sit-ins.html.

p. 36, "I can't even . . ." Beth Strohben, "The Greensboro Four," North Carolina Museum of History, http:// ncmuseumofhistory.org/workshops/legends/Session4.html.

p. 38, "have been complacent . . ." Marvin Sykes, "Negro college students sit at Woolworth lunch counter," *Greensboro Daily News,* February 2, 1960, http://www. sitins.com/headline_sitdown.shtml.

p. 38, "if any legal . . ." Ibid.

p. 39, "No service was . . ." "Movement by Negroes Growing," *Greensboro Daily News,* February 4, 1960, http://www.sitins.com/clipping_020460.shtml.

p. 39, "The doors opened . . ." Sanford Wexler, *An Eyewitness History of the Civil Rights Movement* (New York: Checkmark Books, 1999), 124-125.

p. 40, "You must tell . . ." Taylor Branch, *Parting the Waters: America in the King Years, 1954-63* (New York: Simon & Schuster, 1988), 273.

p. 41, "What are you . . ." Williams, *Eyes on the Prize,* 129.

p. 42, "Here were the . . ." Richard K. Scher, *Politics in the New South: Republicanism, Race, and Leadership in the Twentieth Century* (Birmingham, Ala.: M. E. Sharpe, 1997), 187.

p. 42, "the democratic and . . ." "Group Asks Protest Support," Associated Press, February 20, 1960, http:// www.sitins.com/clipping_022060.shtml.

p. 43, "We are attempting . . ." Ibid.

p. 44, "Negroes, who are . . ." Charles A. Simmons,
*The African American Press: With Special Reference in
Four Newspapers, 1827-1965* (Jefferson, N.C.: McFarland,
1998), 99.

p. 44, "What is fresh . . ." Branch, *Parting the Waters,* 276.

CHAPTER FOUR: "Ins" Across the South

p. 46, "[T]hey were not . . ." Henry Hampton and Steve
Fayer, *Voices of Freedom: An Oral History of the Civil
Rights Movement from the 1950s through the 1980s*
(New York: Bantam Books, 1991), 54.

p. 47, "The first sit-in . . ." Williams, *Eyes on the Prize,* 132.

p. 49, "a group of . . ." Hampton and Fayer, *Voices of
Freedom,* 58.

p. 49, "A group of . . ." Ibid.

p. 50, "[The police] were . . ." "Ain't Scared of Your Jails
(1960-1961)," *PBS,* http://www.pbs.org/wgbh/amex/
eyesontheprize/about/pt_103.html.

p. 51, "You could roll . . ." Williams, *Eyes on the Prize,* 135.

p. 52, "[T]hey simply stood . . ." Hampton and Fayer, *Voices
of Freedom,* 65-66.

p. 52, "wrong to discriminate . . ." Peter Ackerman and
Jack DuVall, *A Force More Powerful: A Century of
Nonviolent Conflict* (New York: Macmillan, 2000), 327.

p. 52, "Mayor, do you . . ." Ibid.

p. 53, "I did not . . ." Susan M. Glisson, *The Human
Tradition in the Civil Rights Movement* (Lanham,
Md.: Rowman & Littlefield, 2006), 176.

p. 54, "Two persons were . . ." Jade Thompson, "Morgan
State Student Activism," http://www.mdcivilrights.
org/MSSA.html.

p. 54, "We'll Walk, Walk . . ." Ibid.

p. 57, "The good nun . . ." "A House Divided Teaching Guide," The Southern Institute for Education and Research, http://www.southerninstitute.info/civil_ rights_education/divided8.html.

p. 58, "Integration Is a . . ." Carson, *Civil Rights Chronicle,* 190.

p. 58, "conscious of a . . ." "Integration Gain Listed by Stores," *New York Times,* October 18, 1960.

p. 58, "Today's youth will . . ." "An Appeal for Human Rights," Civil Rights Movement Veterans, http://www. crmvet.org/docs/aa4hr.htm.

p. 60, "You can't do . . ." Carson, *Civil Rights Chronicle,* 264.

CHAPTER FIVE: Prelude to the Freedom Rides

p. 62, "[The sheriff deputy] . . ." Richard Goldstein, "Irene Morgan Kirkaldy, 90, Rights Pioneer, Dies," *New York Times,* August 13, 2007.

p. 64, "disobedience movement on . . ." "Congress of Racial Equality — CORE," AfricanAmericans.com, http:// africanamericans.com/CongressofRacialEquality.htm.

p. 65-66, *You don't have* . . . "The Journey," RobinWashington. com, http://www.robinwashington.com/jimcrow/2_ journey.html.

p. 66, "coming down here . . ." Arsenault, *Freedom Riders,* 46.

p. 66, "It's about time . . ." "George M. Houser," CORE, http://www.core-online.org/History/george_houser.htm.

p. 67, "The Journey of . . ." Arsenault, *Freedom Riders,* 52.

CHAPTER SIX: Freedom Rides

p. 68, "Until then, I . . ." "James Farmer, Civil Rights Giant in the 50's and 60's," InterChange, http://www.interchange. org/jfarmer.html.

p. 69, "Interstate passengers have . . ." Colin Evans, "Boynton v. Virginia: 1960 — Court Splits, But For Boynton," Law Library, http://law.jrank.org/pages/3094/Boynton-v-Virginia- 1960-Court-Splits-but-Boynton.html.

p. 71, "the movement on . . ." Arsenault, *Freedom Riders,* 94.

p. 72, "We felt that . . ." Hampton and Steve Fayer, *Voices of Freedom,* 75.

p. 74, "You will never . . ." "Freedom Rides," *New Georgia Encyclopedia*, http://www.georgiaencyclopedia.org/nge/Article.jsp?id=h-3618.

p. 75, "dirty Communists . . ." Arsenault, *Freedom Riders,* 143.

p. 76, "Burn them alive . . ." Ibid., 145.

p. 77, "We got clobbered . . ." Hampton and Steve Fayer, *Voices of Freedom,* 78.

p. 78, "that nonviolence can . . ." Williams, *Eyes on the Prize,* 149.

p. 79, "If the Freedom . . ." Ibid.

p. 80, "The people of . . ." Williams, *Eyes on the Prize,* 152.

p. 81, "Kill the nigger-lovin' . . ." Thomas R. Brooks, *Walls Come Tumbling Down: A History of the Civil Rights Movement – 1940-1970* (Englewood Cliffs, N.J.: Prentice-Hall, 1974), 163.

p. 82, "The mob turned . . ." Wexler, *An Eyewitness History of the Civil Rights Movement,* 131.

p. 82, "People with no . . ." Brooks, *Walls Come Tumbling Down,* 163.

p. 83, "Whatever one's views . . ." Wexler, *An Eyewitness History of the Civil Rights Movement,* 132.

p. 84, "If they don't . . ." Branch, *Parting the Waters,* 460.

p. 84, "I think the . . ." Williams, *Eyes on the Prize,* 158.

p. 85, "Freedom Riders must . . ." Branch, *Parting the Waters,* 468.

p. 86, "I sincerely wish . . ." Arsenault, *Freedom Riders,* 262.

p. 87, "I was hit . . ." Carson, *Civil Rights Chronicle,* 198.

p. 89, "They seek an . . ." Peter Macdonald, *Giáp: The Victor in Vietnam* (New York: W. W. Norton, 1993), 184.

p. 92, "He's a gah-damned . . ." Carson, *Civil Rights Chronicle,* 199.

p. 91, "crushed my every . . ." Ibid.

p. 92, "How do you . . ." Ibid.

p. 92, "In my judgment . . ." Wexler, *An Eyewitness History of the Civil Rights Movement,* 134.

CHAPTER SEVEN: A Lasting Impact

p. 94-95, "Sometimes we'd walk . . ." Wexler, *An Eyewitness History of the Civil Rights Movement,* 138.

p. 97, "This is no . . ." "The I Have a Dream Speech," U.S. Constitution Online, http://www.usconstitution. net/dream.html.

p. 97, "Some of you . . ." Ibid.

p. 98, "We must say . . ." "Patience is a Dirty and Nasty Word," PBS, http://www.pbs.org/wgbh/amex/eyesontheprize/ sources/ps_washington.html.

p. 99, "I have always . . ." Deborah Rand, interview with author, September 9, 2006.

p. 100, "I saw a . . ." Kay Michener, interview with author, October 5, 2006.

p. 103, "Last summer I . . ." David Farber, primary consultant, *The Sixties Chronicle* (Lincolnwood, Ill.: Legacy Publishing, 2004), 203.

p. 104, "[W]e lived through . . ." Lorraine Ahearn, "Ambassador Says Sit-ins Inspired South Africans," Greensboro Sit-Ins, February 11, 1996, http://www.sitins. com/headline_021196.shtml.

p. 105, "If America don't . . ." Farber, *The Sixties Chronicle,* 326.

p. 108, "Great people don't . . ." Jim Schlosser, "Courage Cast in Bronze," Greensboro Sit-ins, February 6, 2001, http://www.sitins.com/headline_020201.shtml.

p. 108, "He would like . . ." Ibid.

Bibliography

Ackerman, Peter, and Jack DuVall. *A Force More Powerful: A Century of Nonviolent Conflict* New York: Macmillan, 2000.

Ahearn, Lorraine. "Ambassador Says Sit-ins Inspired South Africans." Greensboro Sit-Ins, February 11, 1996. http://www.sitins.com/headline_021196.shtml.

"Ain't Scared of Your Jails (1960-1961)." PBS. http://www.pbs.org/wgbh/amex/eyesontheprize/about/pt_103.html.

"An Appeal for Human Rights." Civil Rights Movement Veterans. http://www.crmvet.org/docs/aa4hr.htm.

Arsenault, Raymond. *Freedom Riders.* New York: Oxford University Press, 2006.

Baldwin, James. *The Price of the Ticket: Collected Nonfiction, 1948-1985.* New York: Macmillan, 1985.

Bausum, Ann. *Freedom Riders: John Lewis and Jim Zwerg on the Front Lines of the Civil Rights Movement.* Washington: National Geographic, 2006.

Boyd, Herb. *We Shall Overcome.* Naperville, Ill.: Sourcebooks, 2004.

"Boynton v. Virginia: 1960—Court Splits, But For Boynton." Law Library. http://law.jrank.org/pages/3094/Boynton-v-Virginia-1960-Court-Splits-but-Boynton.html.

Branch, Taylor. *Parting the Waters: America in the King Years, 1954-63.* New York: Simon & Schuster, 1988.

Brooks, Thomas R. *Walls Come Tumbling Down: A History of the Civil Rights Movement — 1940-1970.* Englewood Cliffs, N.J.: Prentice-Hall, 1974.

Carson, Clayborne, primary consultant. *Civil Rights Chronicle: The African-American Struggle for Freedom.* Lincolnwood, Ill.: Legacy Publishing, 2003.

Chapelle, Tony. "Adam Clayton Powell, Jr.." *Black Collegian.* http://www.black-collegian.com/african/adam.shtml.

"Congress of Racial Equality — CORE." AfricanAmericans.com. http://africanamericans.com/CongressofRacialEquality.htm.

Cozzens, Lisa. "Sit-in." June 22, 1998, http://www.watson.org/~lisa/blackhistory/civilrights-55-65/sit-ins.html.

Eckels, Carla. "Kansas Sit-In Gets Its Due at Last." NPR, October 21, 2006. http://www.npr.org/templates/story/story.php?storyId=6355095.

"The Emancipation Proclamation." National Park Service. http://www.nps.gov/ncro/anti/emancipation.html.

Farber, David, primary consultant. *The Sixties Chronicle.* Lincolnwood, Ill.: Legacy Publishing, 2004.

"Freedom Rides." *New Georgia Encyclopedia.* http://www.georgiaencyclopedia.org/nge/Article.jsp?id=h-3618.

"George M. Houser." CORE. http://www.core-online.org/History/george_houser.htm.

Glisson, Susan M. *The Human Tradition in the Civil Rights Movement.* Lanham, Md.: Rowman & Littlefield, 2006.

Goldstein, Richard. "Irene Morgan Kirkaldy, 90, Rights Pioneer, Dies." *New York Times,* August 13, 2007.

Goodwin, Jeff, and James M. Jasper. *The Social Movements Reader: Cases and Concepts.* Oxford, England: Blackwell Publishing, 2003.

"Group Asks Protest Support." Associated Press, February 20, 1960, http://www.sitins.com/clipping_022060.shtml.

Halberstam, David. *The Children*. New York: Ballantine Books, 1999.

Hampton, Henry, and Steve Fayer. *Voices of Freedom: An Oral History of the Civil Rights Movement from the 1950s through the 1980s*. New York: Bantam Books, 1991.

"A House Divided Teaching Guide." The Southern Institute for Education and Research. http://www.southerninstitute. info/civil_rights_education/divided8.html.

"The I Have a Dream Speech." U.S. Constitution Online. http://www.usconstitution.net/dream.html.

"Integration Gain Listed by Stores." *New York Times,* October 18, 1960.

"James Farmer, Civil Rights Giant in the 50's and 60's." InterChange. http://www.interchange.org/jfarmer.html.

"James Farmer: Civil Rights Pioneer Farmer Dies." Associated Press. http://www.angelarose.com/FamousDiabetics/ Fam-Political.htm.

"The Journey." http://www.robinwashington.com/jimcrow/ 2_journey.html.

Macdonald, Peter. *Giáp: The Victor in Vietnam*. New York: W. W. Norton, 1993.

"Movement by Negroes Growing." *Greensboro Daily News,* February 4, 1960. http://www.sitins.com/ clipping_020460.shtml.

Murray, Pauli. *Proud Shoes: The Story of an American Family*. Beacon Press, 1999.

"The 1963 Inaugural Address of Governor George C. Wallace." Alabama Department of Archives and History. http://www.archives.state.al.us/govs_list/inauguralspeech. html.

Norris, Michele. "The Woolworth Sit-In That Launched a Movement." NPR. February 1, 2008, http://www.npr.org/templates/story/story.php?storyId=18615556.

"Our Mission." NAACP. http://www.naacp.org/about/mission.

"Patience is a Dirty and Nasty Word." PBS. http://www.pbs.org/wgbh/amex/eyesontheprize/sources/ps_washington.html.

Rozier Albert L. Jr., "Students Hit Woolworth's for Lunch Service." *Register,* February 5, 1960.

Scher, Richard K. *Politics in the New South: Republicanism, Race, and Leadership in the Twentieth Century.* Birmingham, Ala.: M. E. Sharpe, 1997.

Schlosser, Jim. "Courage Cast in Bronze." Greensboro Sit-ins, February 6, 2001. http://www.sitins.com/headline_020201.shtml.

Simmons, Charles A. *The African American Press: With Special Reference in Four Newspapers, 1827-1965.* Jefferson, N.C.: McFarland, 1998.

Simons, William M., and Alvin L. Hall. *The Cooperstown Symposium on Baseball and American Culture.* Jefferson, N.C.: McFarland, 2001.

Strohben, Beth. "The Greensboro Four." North Carolina Museum of History. http://ncmuseumofhistory.org/workshops/legends/Session4.html.

Sykes, Marvin. "Negro college students sit at Woolworth lunch counter." *Greensboro Daily News,* February 2, 1960. http://www.sitins.com/headline_sitdown.shtml.

"Theodore G. Bilbo and the Decline of Public Racism, 1938-1947." *Democratic Underground.* http://www.democraticunderground.com/discuss/duboard.php?az=show_mesg&forum=132&topic_id=4097733&mesg_id=4097733.

Thompson, Jade. "Morgan State Student Activism." http://
www.mdcivilrights.org/MSSA.html.

"United States and American History: Early 1960."
Trivia-Library. http://www.trivia-library.com/a/
united-states-and-american-history-early-1960.htm.

Wexler, Sanford. *An Eyewitness History of the Civil
Rights Movement.* New York: Checkmark Books, 1999.

Williams, Juan. *Eyes on the Prize.* New York: Penguin
Books, 1987.

Winslow, Olivia. "The Fight for Civil Rights: In their
own words." *Newsday.* http://www.newsday.com/
news/nationworld/ny-lfciv0203-pg,0,4117347.
photogallery?index=8.

Wolff, Miles. *How It All Began: The Greensboro Sit-Ins.*
New York: Stein & Day, 1971.

Web sites

http://www.sitins.com/index.shtml
Web site about the Greensboro sit-ins, with pictures, a time-line, and audio clips of the original participants discussing what happened.

http://www.freedomridersfoundation.org/index.html
The Freedom Riders' 40th reunion, which occurred in 2001. Oral histories of the Freedom Rides from participants, and many images and articles.

http://www.naacp.org/
The Web site of the National Association for the Advancement of Colored People. Contains information about the history of the civil rights movement, alerts about contemporary hate crimes, and ways people can get involved to make a difference.

http://www.civilrightsmuseum.org/about/about.asp
Web site of the National Civil Rights Museum. Features pages about the sit-ins and Freedom Rides, and information about the museum, located in Memphis, Tennessee.

Index